UNDERSTANDING

the

GREAT COMMISSION

A Missionary's Thoughts
on the Great Commission

Jon Nelms

ISBN: 978-1-7369574-1-7

First Printing—April 2021

FINAL FRONTIERS FOUNDATION
1200 Peachtree Street • Louisville, GA 30434
800-522-4324 • www.finalfrontiers.org

Scriptures are taken from the King James Bible.

To order additional books, contact:
www.TheGreatOmission.com

Printed and Bound in the United States

Dedication

I DEDICATE THIS work to those who have been with me in my trials and errors, who have helped me learn missions and learn how to teach it to others. You are my inspiration, encouragement, and, in many ways, you are my mentors, taking the rubble I have left in your care and turning it into a fortress.

My son, Daniel Nelms, and his wife, Nolvia.

My daughter, Sara Horne, and her husband, Michael.

My wife Juanita who was beside me from the beginning until she passed to Glory in 2006.

And to my wife Nolin, who is always beside me wherever I go, until I finally go Home.

Table of Contents

Foreword

THE PURPOSE OF this book is to stimulate your thoughts on the subjects of missionaries and missions.

I want you to stand back, as if in an art gallery, and think about what you see. What were the strokes of the artist's brush trying to capture, emphasize, or even disqualify? Is the painting understandable or confusing? Does it inspire, or is it tiresome?

Think of Leutze Wall's painting of Washington crossing the Delaware River. Your first glance will likely fix on the stoic expression on Washington's face. With closer study, you may see the skies clearing on the eastern shore while the storm rages on the western. Did you notice the Scotsman using his oar to move ice chunks away from the boat's port? What about the frontiersman behind him and the freed slave to his right? Did you notice their struggle propelling the boat through the waters, the wind chapping their faces or the scores of others waiting in the background? We know their sufferings and the victory they won, but we don't know how it felt to be there because we were not there.

So, too, our Lord has painted a commission for us to accomplish. A glance will not reveal all that has, is, and must be done to get across the river. Getting in the boat with our Commander is not enough; we need to get to the other side, accomplishing what He commissioned us to accomplish. We know how others have suffered, endured, and conquered, but unless we get in the boat with them, we will never know how it felt. Someday in eternity, we may enjoy a painting of His Commission in a heavenly museum. When that day comes, will you stare in amazement, saying, "Look what they did for Him," or will you gloriously proclaim, "Look what we did for Him!"

A few years ago, my son Daniel conducted an Internet search to see what people are looking for when they" google" the term missions or missionary. The number-one entry was "What is a missionary?"

I would have thought the answer to that question was common sense, but I was wrong. At the same time we discovered this tidbit of information, we were beginning to produce a podcast for our ministry. I then decided to do a two-minute segment at the end of each broadcast to answer those questions.

After developing 54 topics on the subject, I divided them into categories and compiled them into a book, adding a few questions or considerations at the end of each, which I call "Points to Ponder." I then titled each short chapter with an explanation of the issue discussed and with the episode number should you want to visit our podcast and hear the delivery.

I want to make you think and see if, together, we can solve these questions.

- What is a missionary?
- Where does he go?
- What does he do?
- How does he live?
- How is he trained?
- How does he train others?
- What is his purpose?

In my previous two books, I deal with these issues in great detail. My intention for this one is to be an easy read, almost in a "devotional format"—not one for every day, but maybe once a week. My goal is to help you direct your attention (or your family or your Sunday school class) to the subject of missions for about five minutes. Hopefully, I have accomplished my purpose to make each subject interesting by being:

- Educational
- Informational
- Inspirational
- Motivational

I hope you are blessed as you read what I have learned from Scripture and experienced in more than three decades of missionary work. Your suggestions, observations and questions are appreciated and will provide me with more food for thought. Please send them to me by email at jnelms@finalfrontiers.org

P.S. Yes, I know there are only 52 weeks in a year, not 54. Now that I am experiencing "senior moments" and sometimes forget what I have read, I threw in a few extra—in case you might need them.

Misunderstandings about the Great Commission

Episodes 18, 21, 27, 28, 35, 42, 46, 50

The Great Commission Is Both a Noun and a Verb

THE GREAT COMMISSION is both a noun and a verb. While you may argue that this may not be technically correct, I think you'll follow where I'm going with this assertion.

What do the following terms have in common: the Boston Marathon, the Louisiana Purchase, and World War II?

All three are recognized as being nouns with a preceding adjective, but I say that they are also *verbs*—action words preceded by an adverb answering how, when, where, why, or to what extent. The words, *marathon, purchase,* and *war,* can also be both nouns and verbs, depending on their usage and context. So can the word *commission.*

As a noun with an adjective, it's not just any commission; it is the GREAT Commission. But would it surprise you to learn that missionaries see the word *commission* as a verb—the action of fulfilling a commission or task given to us by our Lord? To what extent does it call us to action? It is His GREAT call to action. If He had told us to go into all the world and empty the trash in every nation, our emphasis would not be on the *trash* but on *emptying* it.

It's like the word *church,* which means "a called-out assembly." Our emphasis is on the noun *assembly,* and so we include the word in our facilities and corporations. Still, if the emphasis was that we are physically and spiritually *called out*, then "church" is a verb. You decide. Are we called to assemble, or do we assemble because we are called? Or both?

To confuse things more, the word *pastor* is also both a noun and a verb. A man is a *pastor* (noun) because he *pastors* (verb) the congregation. And sometimes churches split because people don't like the way the pastor (noun) *pastors* (verb).

Perhaps if we saw our congregations less as a noun and more as a verb, then *church* would not simply be a place you go (noun—an assembly) but something you do, i.e., *assemble* (a verb).

A different view of "missions" would be helpful also. If we, the called and assembled, understood that missions is not a project to be highlighted by an annual conference, but the very purpose for being called out, we would doubtless be more dedicated.

Points to Ponder

- The word *Christian* (a noun) arose as a term used to describe those in Antioch at Paul's home church, who were *living like Christ* (an action). In what ways were they Christ-like?

- How do you demonstrate a Christlikeness?

- What attributes of your lifestyle could be changed to make you more like Christ?

The Great Commission Is About Reaching Nations—Not Countries

WHEN I WAS a young boy, we would hear stories about the Cherokee and Apache Nations. I thought the words *nation* and *country* were always synonymous, but I was wrong.

A *country* is "a geographical, political area with a government, a monetary system, a flag, unique laws, etc." It is a unified territory with established borders.

A *nation* is "a unique 'people group,' with both a common DNA and culture," which though similar, stand out as distinct from every other people group on the planet.

Shortly after World War II, theologians rushed to announce the Great Commission had finally been fulfilled. They reasoned that Christian soldiers had visited every unreached nation in the world by the war's end, proclaiming the gospel as they went. Then some began to realize that our understanding of the verse was incorrect. The Great Commission does not compel us to evangelize geo/political regions but rather ethnic groups. The job was not completed then or now, as at least 6,000 unreached ethnic groups are still known to exist worldwide.

The Greek word used in the Great Commission for "nation" is *ethnos*, the word from which our modern term, *ethnic groups* is derived. The Scots, for example, are an ethnic group. Still, the wording used to describe heaven's choir in Revelation 7:9 would emphasize evangelizing not only Scotland as a country or the Scots as a race, but also each separate clan (or family) of the Scots. We are, therefore, to reach even the MacAllisters, the MacDonalds and the MacLeods.

The Cherokee *ethnos* ("people, nation") long inhabiting the Eastern United States were forcibly moved to Oklahoma, but they didn't cease to be Cherokees. The Apaches were moved to Mexico, Oklahoma, and Florida, but they were still Apaches. You can change your country, and you can successfully assimilate into a different culture—that's what immigration is all about. You cannot change your DNA, and *that* is what the Great Commission is all about.

Points to Ponder

- Do you know which *ethnos* make up your family?

- Has your *ethnos*, as a whole, been exposed to the gospel?

- Do other members of your *ethnos* live nearby?

- How can you influence them for Christ?

The Great Commission and the Diaspora

S INCE THE GREAT Commission is about going into all the world, why do we talk about sending others rather than going ourselves? Especially consider other verses that adequately emphasize the "sending" aspect.

Some say Christ was speaking prophetically about the future sacking of Jerusalem. In other words, they feel He was telling them on that day some thirty years in the future when they will be scattered while fleeing the destruction of the Roman forces, they should be sure to witness everywhere they go. I doubt that interpretation, and so did Paul, Barnabas, Silas, and many others. After all, He did tell them to delay— not for thirty years, but for the Holy Spirit's arrival, fifty days later.

The truth is Christ gave His devout Jewish followers a task that they failed to obey. Some say that the Jews needed to be dispersed before the disciples could spread out to reach them. That assumption is not true since they had already been dispersed for a thousand years.

In 562 BC, Jews living in Cochin, India, established a trading post there. They had settled there during Solomon's reign to traffic in teakwood, ivory, spices, and peacocks. In 700 BC, Sennacherib seized some 200,000 Jews, forcibly moving them to southern Turkey and northern Iraq, and in 600 BC, Nebuchadnezzar enslaved tens of thousands, taking them to Iraq and Persia (Iran). In 200 BC, they were traveling the Silk Road and trading with the Han dynasty in China. A decade before Julius Caesar's rule, Governor Lucius Valerius Flaccus stated that the Jewish population of Asia Minor numbered at least 180,000 persons. In 27 BC, over 8,000 Jews lived in Rome, and according to some historians, their number comprised as much as ten percent of the city's population. Finally, Philo, who lived at that time in Alexandria, wrote that more than one million Jews lived in Egypt, one-eighth of the population.

Those who understood that the commission of Christ deserved and required their immediate and full attention decided not to wait but proceed as best they could, fulfilling the task and trusting God to make the best of their labors. The fruit that remains they produced includes both you and me. The others jumped on board later, but the old saying, "better late than never," applies to both them and to us.

Points to Ponder

- The term *diaspora* does not define one particular dispersal of the Jews (AD 70) but any and every dispersal, including Jacob's moving his family to Egypt and Moses leading them out to Canaan.

- What modern-day diasporas (i.e., refugees) have you witnessed? How have past diasporas influenced your community?

- Did you know when people arrive in their new homeland, they are most acceptable to hear the "good news" of Jesus Christ from a friendly citizen? How can you share the gospel with them?

The Great Commission Repeated

W AS THE GREAT Commission given only once? In Mark 16:7, while still in the garden tomb area, Jesus instructed Mary to tell the disciples to meet Him at a designated place in Galilee. And Matthew 28:16-18 records the proclamation taking place on a mountaintop—*in* Galilee. But Luke 24:50 tells us that He spent His final hours with His disciples in Jerusalem, then walked with them as far as Bethany, and from there He ascended. His final words that we call the Great Commission were His parting words.

When He sent out the disciples to evangelize, He may have often repeated the command to encourage and embolden as He reminded them of the purpose of His sending. Besides the references already mentioned, common sense would suggest that if this commission was important enough to be His last words, they were important enough to have been spoken many times—not hidden in a secret place of His heart to be reserved as a one-time, parting command. After all, how many times do you tell your wife that you love her? Often, I hope, because if those words are being reserved as your final words, then you may be saying them sooner than you think!

What Christ said is more important than where He said it, when He said it, or how often He may have said it. In a dozen or so words,

He shares eight specific details:

1. Who the sender is—Himself, not a board, a church or a denomination

2. Whose authority He is sending with—His Father's

3. What power He is sending with—all the power given to Him in the totality of His creation

4. Who He is sending—us

5. Where He is sending us—to the entire world

6. What He is sending us to do—to preach the Gospel

7. Who will accompany us—He and His Holy Spirit

8. And finally, how long He will accompany us—until the end of the earth

No business or battle plan conceived by man has ever been so expansive and, at the same time, so concise. On the other hand, no other command of God, existing for over two thousand years, remains yet to be obeyed. The shame is not His; it is ours. Let's get busy and obey.

Points to Ponder

- If we will not obey it, does it matter how many times or in how many locations Christ may have repeated this command?

- In your life with your time, talents and financial means, what have you done to help fulfill His Commission? What else or what more could you do?

- If an observer studied your life and actions, would he surmise that you view Christ's words as a *Great Commission* you obey or as a *Mediocre Suggestion* you ignore?

Feeding the 5000
and the Great Commission

ESUS ONCE PREACHED to an outdoor assembly of 5,000 men plus
the women and children. If 5,000 men would forfeit their wages
by walking off their job for an entire day, one can only imagine how
the crowd must have increased with the addition of the homebound
women, children, and servants.

After teaching for hours, our Lord paused to feed the crowd. Since
His team had not brought food, they searched to gather whatever was
available. They found a young boy whose mother had provided him
with five pieces of what was probably flatbread and two small fish,
most likely roasted or grilled.

Jesus multiplied that boy's lunch, providing enough for everyone
to eat and then told His disciples to pass out the food. Imagine how
long such a task would take and how repetitively tedious it would have
been for the disciples. But what if the disciples had misunderstood
His command, thinking our Lord's intention was simply to distribute
the food instead of providing portions for ALL the people present?
What if the disciples then had logically passed out the first portions to
those who sat nearest the Lord, then gathered more and went back to
giving food to the same people again and again until it was all gone?
Those fortunate few in the front would have been gluttonous, eating

more than they needed and hoarding what they did not. The misunderstanding would have sufficiently supplied them with the ability to open their own bakeries and fish restaurants with the surplus they had received. In contrast, thousands of others would have gone away hungry and empty-handed. So, we see that understanding the Lord's intention was vital to fulfilling His purpose!

Speaking of intent and purpose...did you know that of every $100 given to churches in America, only one dollar goes to missions? We consume the $99 on ourselves, and then, hoarding the abundance, we pray with our hands up, not out, asking for more. We commandeer the abundance God meant for others and consume it on our own desires. And what of the $1 that does go to missions? Incredibly, 90¢ of the $1 is used to support missionaries serving in areas already saturated with the gospel. Only 10¢ of every $100 go to help give the Bread of Life to those who have never heard His name. When Christ gave us the Great Commission, He did not have in mind only taking the gospel to the front row of Palestine but to all the world—even for those sitting in the back.

Points to Ponder

- Considering we have yet to obey His command, do you suppose the front rows may be overweight with gospel consumption while others starve without it?

- What can you do to deliver the Bread of Life to those who only see it from a distance but hunger for a taste?

- While some today disagree with using food, health care, etc., as a tool to present the gospel in an embracing way, Jesus did so all the time. Was He wrong? How do His actions influence your view of helping as well as preaching?

In the Great Commission, We Emphasize the Going and Sending— Not the Preaching

W E ARE ALL zealous about the Great Commission, which is why our churches have mission conferences and give so generously for the cause. But sometimes, we may forget the purpose behind our commission. Some are eager to go and others to send, but the commission is actually about more than merely going or sending.

When you plan a vacation to Disney World, in what are you and your family primarily interested? Is it putting aside the funds you need, the adventure of the journey, or arriving at the park? You could argue all the planning and preparation is necessary to the process. But what you and the kids are really thinking about is the Magic Kingdom, Space Mountain, Pirates of the Caribbean, Thunder Mountain, and the other rides; or if you're like me, all the theme restaurants at Epcot Center.

With missions, going and sending, though necessary, are the prelude to what the Greatest of Commissions is all about. I have seen many missionaries struggle for years to get to the field. As a result, it seems to be such a landmark in their journey that when they hop off the airplane, they declare "mission accomplished." That didn't work for President Bush, and it doesn't work for us either. Simply getting to the field should not be the goal; rather, it's only the first step in a lifelong journey.

Every step we take on our mission's adventure is necessary. There is a purpose for deputation, and a purpose for the going and the sending; however, it is not simply to get us there. The steps taken are to enable us, once we are there, to preach the gospel of Jesus Christ, disciple the converts, plant churches and train pastors who will do the same.

We are all on the same team, and each team member has a specific part to play—even the water boy and the cheerleaders. We all have the same purpose and goal. That goal is not to arrive at the stadium, it is not to wear a uniform or impress the fans, and it is not to play with all our might. The ultimate goal is to win. Let's remember what the Great Commission is all about...and let's get the job done.

Points to Ponder

- We often see a missionary finally arriving on the field as the "end of the means" rather than as "a means to the end." How do you view it?

- Since we are to "preach the gospel," should we support missionaries who are not involved with preaching? Wouldn't it be better to support them as ministers doing ministry rather than as missionaries planting churches?

- How can we be more effective as senders and become more eager as goers?

Is a Church a Building
or a Congregation?

OUR MINISTRY OF supporting national church planters is quite effective. Some consider the numbers of conversions and the new churches planted astounding. In contrast, others dismiss them as unbelievable. I think the primary reason is they do not understand what a church is.

In our American culture when we hear the term "church," we think of a building. (Go on now, admit it.) We know that is not technically correct, but that image has become so ingrained in us that we even refer to the building as being the "church" or "God's House." We know full well that the church is not the building—but our bodies that are the temples of God. We don't think of church as worshippers, but as a "place of worship" with property, a baptistry, pews, a pulpit, a choir (robes optional), songbooks, and even a parking lot, signboard, offices, and a fellowship hall with a full kitchen.

A church is neither a location nor a facility; it is a congregation. At Final Frontiers, we define a *church* as "a group of newly saved and baptized believers meeting together regularly for worship, under the leadership of a pastor." The Bible refers to these congregations meeting in homes as "churches." In each epistle, they have:

1. a place to meet—someone's house

2. a pastor or several of them

3. a people—a congregation of newly saved and baptized believers

Some churches, like Corinth, even had backslidden and unsaved participants meeting with, and at times, leading them. The church addressed in III John had a greedy and ungodly pastor who refused to allow the congregation to assist missionaries and cast out members who did so anyway. No church is perfect because no people are perfect—even if their building is.

Typically, our "churches" start in a home, on a front porch, or under a tree. In time they acquire the trappings of what we in America call churches, but for the most part, they spend their tithes supporting their pastors, caring for the needy (saved and unsaved), and evangelizing the lost. And that's why statistically (2020), they report a new convert every 23 seconds, and a new church started every 16 minutes. How's that for astounding?

Points to Ponder

- I know you know, but honestly, don't you often think of "the church" as the building where you worship? I do.

- What other misconceptions might we have and pass down to our children?

- Might it be wiser to emphasize facilities (and their costs) less and evangelizing and care-giving more? How can you accomplish that in your life?

More Lessons
from Feeding the Masses

W E ALL KNOW that on one occasion Christ fed 5,000 men, plus the women and children (Matthew 14), and on another occasion, 4,000 men, plus the women and children were fed (Mark 8).

Our Lord could have fed every hungry person on earth if He wanted, but He responded to those who followed Him. On both occasions, though the people were seeking, they were not starving or even close to it; they were simply hungry from not having eaten all day. In these two cases, our Lord was not responding to a crisis but to a need. Regarding salvation, though every man needs to hear the gospel, the closer a person gets to the end of his or her days, the more that need becomes a crisis.

On these two occasions, we also see an important lesson: if a need exists, and our Lord has taken the time to supply that need, then we have the responsibility to disperse His supply and meet that need. Otherwise, His provision was in vain. Imagine, after multiplying the food for all to partake, the disciples stood back, beheld the crowd, and reasoned, "This is just too much work for the few of us. We need to organize a conference and bring in other disciples gifted at serving; after all, our gifts lay in teaching and administration." Had that logic guided their decision, the food would have rotted before they could have printed the conference fliers.

"That's silly," some would say. But is it? Did you know that Christians spend more money planning, promoting, and attending mission conferences than they actually give to missions?! We put more effort into weaving the baskets than we do in using them to feed the spiritually hungry. Christ did not tell us to go into all the world to strategize; He told us to evangelize.

Christ did His part by gathering the crowd and providing the food. We are to do our part by using what He has provided to fulfill the Great Commission. And yes, some do have the gift of serving, but all of us should be able to pass out a simple evangelistic "happy meal" to those who are spiritually hungry.

Points to Ponder

- Why, as humans, do we wait for a crisis to do what we knew already needed to be done?

- What excuses do we give for not distributing the Bread of Life?

- How can we shift from being basket weavers to food distributors?

Great Commission Successes

Episodes 40, 41, 45

Chinese Churches
Swell Without Missionaries

A DECADE BEFORE World War II, missionaries were forced to leave China. They were blamed for their homeland's political and military sins and were called "white devils," who were only there to corrupt young minds and destroy old traditions with their introduction of a foreign god. Those who left too slowly were arrested, tortured, and martyred. This sudden missionary exodus caused believers in Europe, America, and the West to bemoan the fact that China would be spiritually doomed without the missionaries. But what they didn't realize was, if a missionary is doing his job and doing it well, he will ultimately make himself irrelevant anyway.

Current mission philosophy teaches that we should pick a city, move there, carefully witness so that we do not alienate ourselves from the government and get deported, and then seek out believers to help us start a new church. Then we should give that congregation 100 percent of our time as their pastor. Ideally, the missionary remains there for twenty or thirty years (though most don't last five). Then he calls his mission board asking them to send his replacement, and he retires. This current modern method teaches our missionaries to become pastors, not missionaries. Believe it or not, that is the typical pattern. So, you see, we haven't fulfilled the Great Commission because we have abandoned the Great Example of how to accomplish God's commission. Fortunately, the earlier missionaries to China had followed the biblical pattern, doing what missionaries were meant to do. They duplicated themselves by creating their own replacements from within the Chinese churches rather than rely on Western replacements.

By 1948, China had been without missionaries for fourteen years and had become a Communist country, with less than one million Christians. Nearly four decades later, when the Bamboo Curtain fell, Western ministries began to return. Their consensus was that during the 40-year absence of missionaries, the Chinese church had grown from less than one million to more than 125 million professing Christians. *Well done, faithful servants!*

Points to Ponder

- Were you aware that there are so many believers in China?

- Did you realize that the massive increase in converts came after the foreign missionaries were expelled? Why do you think that is?

- Paul told his disciples to "teach others" who will be able to do likewise, setting up a never-ending cycle. How effective were the early missionaries at following that directive, and how can we encourage others to do the same?

- This is discipleship in its purest form. Are you discipling anyone, or will the cycle end with you? You don't know what you can teach? Teach anything you know to anyone who doesn't know.

More Elephants than Christians

WHEN I FIRST went to Thailand in 1986, there were not many Christians there. Due to Adoniram Judson's ministry right across the Burmese border, Baptist missionaries first arrived in 1833. Seven years later, Presbyterian missionaries arrived, as well as a small contingent of Chinese missionaries. Following them were Burmese missionaries from the Karen tribe (pronounced *Ca-reen*). Associates of Judson had mostly converted their tribe, and they were eager to share their new faith with their tribal cousins in Thailand. Sixty-five years later, in 1868, the first Western-style church was organized in the northern city of Chiang Mai, the seat of the "hill tribe" region, and a year later, the first two Thai Christians were martyred there. Flash forward.

In 1986, the Thai government's estimate of the Christian population was only .01 percent. They openly boasted that Thailand had more elephants than Christians. Until the 1990s, most believers were tribal, except for a significant percentage of the young medical professionals, who foreign medical teams had heavily evangelized.

Twenty-four years later in the 2000 census, 0.7 percent of the total population of 60 million were registered as Christians. Today (2020) that number has grown to as much as 2 percent.

That percentage equates to nearly 1,200,000 converts still living after three decades. With only 20 Independent Baptist missionaries and relatively few from other groups serving there, this means that the national church and the national and tribal preachers have risen to carry the load of reaching their country. That's a success story!

Still, 57 percent of all Christians in Thailand live in the northern provinces (the "hill tribe" regions), and 51 percent of all Christians live in only three predominantly tribal provinces where Judson's Baptist disciples started 185 years ago. In most countries, such as Mexico, Brazil, and Peru, missionaries overlook the tribal people to reach the citizens. Thailand, however, is an enigma, where, to the contrary, we have overlooked the citizens to reach the tribal groups. Nevertheless, the good news is, there are now more Christians in Thailand than there are elephants.

Points to Ponder

- Were you aware that Adoniram Judson had produced so much "fruit that remained?"

- I have spent well over a year of my life in Thailand. During that time, I saw only two elephants. Since there were more elephants than Christians at that time, that means as I walked the streets of the country, it is likely that I never passed a Christian.

- Why do you suppose the Thai convert so slowly and the tribal peoples more rapidly? The answer: Many of their tribal legends parallel the stories of the Bible. They say they once had "a book" about the Creator, but their forefathers lost it. They have been waiting for it to return, and now it has. (Read the introduction of my book, *The Great Omission*, to learn more.)

The Shock and Awe
of Pentecost

"SHOCK AND AWE" is one of the mightiest tools of the military. Typically, this tactic is not employed at the end of the war but at the beginning. It is an opportunity for the offense to display their strength in hopes of achieving a swift surrender by crippling the enemy's ability to move about, produce armaments, and resupply their troops.

On Pentecost, our Lord shook His enemy so severely that Satan was paralyzed and unable to stop what was occurring. Sure, he must have expected something, but he didn't see *that* coming! Christ had departed, leaving the promise of sending His Spirit to take His place. Now, rather than Christ walking side by side with a few believers, His Spirit would come "alongside" *every* believer, empowering them (us) to rain down spiritual shock and awe around the world.

His weapon was His Word, His power was His Spirit, and His troops were His converts. That day, when His Spirit fell on His followers, a powerful shock and awe was released that continues worldwide even today.

His Spirit gave us wisdom, guidance, instruction, and power. He supplies each of us, not with off-the-rack armor, but with the armor of God Himself, tailored to fit each of us. Every piece is custom designed to make us effective and invincible warriors, before whom the gates of hell will fall, and the infantry of hell will flee. We don't even have defensive armor because God *never* retreats. When Peter was fitted with God's armor and preached in the power of God's Spirit, spiritual shock and awe bombarded hell and earth, as men from multiple nations miraculously heard "the marvelous works of God" in their own languages.

Pentecost was the shock and awe in a war called the Great Commission. It was not the end of the war; it was the beginning, and it still rages today. We at home need to do our part to supply and resupply our troops worldwide, both the foreign and national missionaries, until the war ends, and we are all honorably discharged.

Points to Ponder

- When fighting our Lord's battles, we are only a casualty if we choose to be.

- Consider this: if we are wearing the armor of God, from a distance, we resemble Him. What great fear that must put in the enemy! I wonder, though, when we get closer in attack mode, do they breathe a sigh of relief or fear our handling of our Lord's mighty sword?

- God wants to use you in His army. Have you enlisted, or are you AWOL?

- Have you learned yet to wield the broadsword of His Word as easily as a fencer's foil? *En garde.*

Can We Fulfill
the Great Commission?

Episodes 5, 12

Using the Internet
to Witness

D ID YOU KNOW that at any given moment 51 percent of the
people online are communicating in either Mandarin Chinese or English? Now let me ask you logically: of the remaining 49 percent who speak other languages, how many of those do you think have a driving desire or need to learn Mandarin compared to learning English?

In these final years before our Lord's return, He has allowed man to conceive and construct a tool whereby any and all of us can literally go into all the world without ever leaving our homes. This Great Commission tool is possibly the Greatest Commission tool; it is called the Internet.

Rather than chatting endlessly on frivolous topics, why not intentionally give a few minutes of your online life to seek out English speakers with whom you can develop a relationship and share the gospel? Make yourself available on sites like ItalkI.com, or those found at www.myenglishteacher.eu/blog/your-top-10-language-exchange-websites-for-speaking-english-fluently

Many students and business professionals are online right now, looking for English speakers to practice conversational English by chatting or texting. Communicating with them daily or weekly will open the door for you to develop a friendship. Your pastor or a good mission board can help you find a missionary in their country with whom, at your recommendation, they can visit and "practice their English face to face." In time, many will gain full exposure to the gospel, profess Christ and become a witness in their land.

The Holy Spirit miraculously connected the evangelist Philip with an Ethiopian civil servant interested in Christ's message. The result was his conversion and the spreading of the gospel throughout his country. If God could use Philip so mightily on the footboards of a chariot, think how He can use you on the keyboard of your computer!

Points to Ponder

- Many people are paid to "tutor" foreign students online, and there are portals you can find that will introduce you to organizations that can help you find students who want to practice their English.

- You are probably contacted frequently by foreigners using Facebook as a means to make friends in America. Some want to scam you, but others only want to talk. Look for foreigners in your "friends" list and contact a few.

- Befriend someone in your area who is obviously a foreigner with communication difficulties. Most will only learn English gradually by gaining exposure to English-speaking people. Befriend one or two. Buy them a coffee and offer to have frequent meetings to talk so that they can learn English. You'll make an instant friend and might make an eternal neighbor. At the very least, you'll be treated to delicious ethnic foods.

How Difficult Is It to Finish the Great Commission?

T HE NEW TESTAMENT "churches" were the body of Christ in a particular geographic area. They were *congregations*—not corporations. Paul wrote to churches in the homes of Philemon in Colossae and Lydia in Philippi. Still, he also wrote to the assembled ones in the Ephesian metropolis, the third largest city of Rome. Corinth evidently had two congregations—Upper Corinth on the hills overlooking the sea inhabited by the wealthy, and Lower Corinth situated on the docks where merchants like Aquila and Priscilla worked in the second largest market of the Empire. Some believe the two Corinthians letters were written individually to each congregation rather than as two letters to both. That would certainly make sense.

Paul also wrote to the churches of Galatia, which was not a city, but a region in what is today Turkey. Those in northern Galatia were not Greeks but were Gauls and Celts. Their ancestors came from the British Isles and northern Europe who had lived there for three centuries. Though considered barbarians due to their ancestry, they spoke Greek and lived under Roman law. The southern Galatians, however, were primarily of Greek ancestry and more easily converted.

Finally, Paul wrote to all the believers in Rome, a church he did not start, stating that he was planning to visit them on his way to Spain.

He was leaving Asia and Greece because he had no place left there to preach. While there were ample places to preach or pastor, he had worked himself out of a job as a church planter in unreached towns. His team had planted churches in every place, which could now finish the job of saturation evangelism; thus, he planned to pass through Rome on his way to Spain's unreached field.

In the first few decades, they had "turned the world upside down." By the year 100, there was one church for every twelve unreached people groups. Today there are more than 416 churches for every one unreached people group. To finish the Great Commission, we don't have to build the entire house; we only need to place the last few bricks on the chimney, and it's done.

Points to Ponder

- Consider that every church in existence was a "house church" until the middle of the third century AD. Take a moment and think about the intimate surroundings, the close-knit relationships, and the atmosphere of "family" rather than "corporate." How is that better or worse than what we have today?

- Paul targeted unreached people groups. We should do the same in our mission efforts.

- Paul was not an architect of churches; he was a contractor. His job was to lay the foundation and let someone else build the "body." He never "built upon another man's foundation."

Missiology and Worlds

Episode 1

Worlds A, B and C

IN MISSIONS, THREE worlds exist today, known as Worlds A, B, and C.

World A is composed of those who have never heard the name of Jesus. They comprise 28 percent of the earth's population and live primarily in tribal groups, strict Islamic lands, and in what is called the 10/40 window. Only 2.5 percent of all existing missionaries are attempting to reach them. Their combined missionary support is equal to only 1¢ of every $100 given to missions.

World B is comprised of those who have limited access to the gospel, though they may have never personally heard it. Thirty-nine percent of the earth's population live in these lands, such as Kenya, Malaysia, Uruguay, and Burma. Only 17.5 percent of all existing missionaries are attempting to reach them. Only 99¢ of every $100 given to missions is designated to finance them.

World C includes those who have both unlimited and unrestricted access to the gospel. They comprise 33 percent of the earth's population and live in countries such as England, America, Germany, and Australia. Incredibly, 80 percent of all existing missionaries are ministering to this group, consuming $99 out of every $100 given to missions.

Knowing these facts, we must ask ourselves the following questions:

Why do we designate the least in manpower and money to reach those who have never heard the gospel?

Why do we give the most to continually evangelize the least who have heard it but seem to ignore it?

Is that how we define "stewardship?"

Perhaps the answer is found in yet another question:

Is the purpose of missions to continually preach the gospel to those who have already heard it or to those who have never yet heard it?

The local church's efforts and tithe are for reaching home. The church's mission giving should be for reaching, not more of the home area, but the unreached world.

Points to Ponder

- Of all the missionaries you know or support, what percentage are working in counties that already have unlimited access to the gospel and have been producing their own pastors for centuries?

- How quickly could we finish the Great Commission task if we sent missionaries to those who have never heard rather than to those whose cultures and language have unlimited exposure?

- The responsibility of the pastor and the local church is to finish the task of evangelizing their community. The missionary's responsibility is to infiltrate unreached communities and create a new body of believers that a pastor can then mature and lead to complete the task.

The Value and Practicality of Supporting National Missionaries

Episodes 2, 4, 38

Working Together to Reach the World by Supporting Nationals

H OW DIFFICULT IS it really to finance the evangelism of the world? That depends on your method of attempting to do it. The Scripture says, "one will chase a thousand, but two will chase ten thousand;" thus, the more of us who work together, the quicker we will get the job done.

Though it takes money to evangelize the world, some still seem to think all we have to do is pray and have good intentions, and then God will do the rest. He indeed can, but He revealed to us that HIS plan is for us to do it—in HIS power, using HIS funding. Paul asked these four questions in Romans chapter ten:

1. How then shall they call on him in whom they have not believed?

2. How shall they believe in him of whom they have not heard?

3. How shall they hear without a preacher?

4. How shall they preach, except they are sent?

So, we can agree that our job is to evangelize the world, but obviously, we cannot all go *somewhere*, and none of us can go *everywhere*; thus, we must send others to accomplish the task. In other words, some give, and others go.

Unfortunately, more countries are closed to missionaries than open, and many languages are yet to be understood, so how can we reach our mandated goal of evangelizing the entire world by using only American missionaries? The fact is, we cannot. Therefore, we must utilize the men God has already placed in each culture to reach their own people; we call these men *national preachers.*

And how can we fund them? It's simple. Many national preachers can survive on as little as $30 a month. If a congregation of 100 people would each give only one penny a day, those combined pennies could support one national preacher full-time. Imagine what that same congregation could accomplish with a quarter a day!

Points to Ponder

- Supporting nationals is an issue of *opportunity.* Every country closed to foreign missionaries is open to national preachers. We reach those we can locally, and we help the nationals reach those we cannot globally.

- Supporting national preachers is an issue of *effectiveness.* They don't have to learn a langue, adapt to a culture, waste years on deputation and furlough, or move their family to live among strangers.

- Supporting nationals is an issue of *economics.* Many can live on $20 a month, others on $200 a month. Compared to American missionaries, the support ratio is as many as 100 national preachers for the same money as one American.

Most Unbelievers
Don't Know a Believer

STATING THAT 100 PERCENT of all unbelievers in the world do not have a relationship with Jesus Christ is redundant, but did you know that 86 percent of all unbelievers also do not have a personal relationship with a Christian? Yet history has demonstrated that friendships and family relationships are the best and surest way to bring a person to Christ.

Andrew brought his brother, Simon Peter, to meet Jesus.

When Hellenic visitors in Jerusalem heard about our Lord raising Lazarus from the dead, they sought out, not Christ Himself, but some of His disciples and requested, *"Sirs, we would see Jesus"* (John 12:21).

When Saul encountered Jesus on the road to Damascus, the Holy Spirit sent Ananias to befriend him, heal him and bring him to a saving knowledge of Christ.

After a businesswoman named Lydia met Paul, Silas, Timothy, and Luke on the banks of a small river outside Philippi, she invited them to her house, became a believer, and her home became the first house church in Europe. While there, Paul and Silas were arrested and got to know a Philippian jailor and his family—more converts. Then there was Peter fellowshipping with and converting the entire household of Cornelius, a Roman centurion. The examples of friendship and family evangelism are endless.

Tragically, there is only a slight chance of someone who does not know a believer ever coming to Christ. It happens, but it is rare. Yet, there is every reason to expect that someone who does know a believer would come to Christ—unless that believer utterly fails in his opportunities to witness.

Most unbelievers don't know a Christian because they live in countries restricted or closed to missionary activity. But God always has a witness on hand. We call them national preachers, and we as a ministry exist to find them and support them. Would you like to help?

Points to Ponder

- How did you first hear about Christ? Was the messenger a stranger or a family member?

- In many cultures, once the family leader comes to Christ, the rest begin to open their hearts and mind to receive the gospel message.

- How meaningful are personal relationships? They influence where we live, where we work, where we attend worship services, what we eat, how we dress, where we shop, where we vacation, our accent, our faith, our political views, etc. They made us who we are and what we will become.

- Believers have to hide their faith in some lands due to persecution, but the Light of the gospel pierces their relationships and is bringing millions to Christ in lands where doing so carries a death sentence.

National Preachers
Are Not Rice Christians

IN 1986, WHEN I began promoting the idea of supporting national preachers to reach their own people, I ran into significant opposition—but not from missionaries. They knew firsthand the advantages the national preachers had in reaching their own families and neighbors. But some mission leaders were opposed to the idea and publicly ridiculed the national preachers, saying they were ignorant or lazy or *rice Christians*—a popular term used to denigrate national preachers, labeling them as insincere servants to any faith that would feed them.

Churches slowly began to accept my arguments on behalf of supporting national missionaries. My assertions were logical, biblical and unarguably effective. Even the apostle Paul did it. Some critics said we were trying to change missions, but we were actually trying to bring it back to its biblical roots. Missions had changed 200 years earlier when mission boards and churches determined that only an American or an European could be supported as a missionary. The national preachers, if helped at all, were relegated to being their drivers and servants. Well-meaning boards created the modern method of missions, and while it has worked, it is not nearly as effective as the biblical method.

After WWII, missionaries flocked to the Philippines, having

served there in the war, and they had fallen in love with the people. Thirty years later, in 1975, their numbers had grown to about 3,000 missionaries, and coincidently, about 3,000 churches as well. But over the next thirty years, death, retirement, and the attraction of other lands saw their numbers decrease. Finally, in 2005, only 118 of the 3,000 remained, yet the number of churches had increased to 55,000.

If it took three decades for 3,000 foreign missionaries to start 3,000 churches—then how in the following three decades could just 118 missionaries start another 52,000 churches? The short answer is they couldn't, and they didn't. The work was done primarily by the nationals they had won to Christ and discipled, who then duplicated the missionaries' efforts and produced a great and expanding harvest—not of rice, but of souls.

Points to Ponder

- Why should anyone serious about the Great Commission reject the willingness of nationals to help?

- What motivation could lead us to say they are unworthy of financial support?

- Since we are all citizens of some country, is it not fair to say that we are all nationals?

- If national preachers should only be supported by their local church, shouldn't that also apply to an American missionary who is also pastoring a local church? If not, why not?

Supporting
Missions Biblically

Episode 36

How Was the Tithe Used in the Early Church?

Tithes and offerings mentioned in the New Testament had a specific purpose. The birth of the church was still recent, and there were not yet any church buildings. It would be nearly 300 more years before the first structure built specifically for the use of Christian worship would be erected. Another 1,100 years would pass after that before someone would think to provide seats for the worshippers.

Based on these historical facts, some say that it is unbiblical to have worship facilities, but they are wrong. Neither Jesus nor the early church had air conditioning, P.A. systems, recorded music, carpet, padded seats, or youth pastors. They also didn't have microwaves, toilets, or cars. If you want to criticize those who worship in a church building, you might want to do it while denouncing the other modern conveniences we all enjoy today.

But to the point, if there were no buildings to erect or remodel, then what were the tithes and offerings used for? The book of Acts and the Epistles disclose that tithes and offerings were explicitly used for three purposes:

1. To care for the widows and orphans

2. To help those in prison and dire need

3. To provide wages and assistance for God's ministerial servants, pastors of local churches, and missionaries to serving worldwide to establish local churches. Third John refers to this purpose.

Does this mean that spending our tithes primarily on real estate and construction is unbiblical? No. However, it would suggest that it is contrary to God's intended purposes if our giving is spent primarily on the organization, the facilities, and programs while failing to provide enough funds or any funds at all on what they were intended for. How tragic when a congregation claims they cannot afford to pay their pastor or cannot afford to give or give more to missions because they have indebtedness to in-house projects which consume their offerings.

How can we say we are doing something for the "glory of God" when we intentionally deny His expressed purposes for those funds in doing so?

Points to Ponder

- The Bible says that Christians were known for their love—not for saying they loved but for demonstrating it—and not exclusively toward other believers, but to the unconverted as well. How can we imitate their actions?

- History tells us that the early "house churches" (as they all were) used their tithes to care for their pastors, support missions, and coordinate relief efforts in their own towns and abroad.

- The early churches did not spend their tithes on themselves but on advancing the cause of Christ. Imagine what churches could accomplish today if we were free to use our tithes on the Great Commission rather than facilities.

What Is a
Mission Field?

Episodes 6, 49, 52, 53

What Is a Mission Field?

WE OFTEN HEAR Christian leaders referring to their towns as a mission field. But why? We promote youth mission trips, then take them to Houston or Miami, where they clean up hurricane debris and pass out water bottles. Biblically, these are *ministries*—not missions. A missionary may give away water, but everyone who gives away water is not a missionary. A pilot may eat a bag of peanuts, but everyone on an airplane who eats a bag of peanuts is not a pilot. Nor is everyone on the plane who works for the airline a pilot. They each have their job to do. And trust me, you don't want an airline attendant in the pilot's seat.

K. P. Yohanan once said that after Pentecost, Jerusalem ceased to be a mission field and became a parish. What is the difference? A mission field is a place primarily populated by people who have never heard the gospel and are likely to have had little or no exposure to it. Paul made this distinction by stating that he, as a missionary, never built upon another man's foundation. Paul almost always preached where no one had gone before him. But why did he limit himself in that way? Because as a missionary, his job description was to take the gospel where it had never been preached before. Once there, he would convert the lost, baptize the new believers, then develop disciples. He would then leave someone behind to pastor the new flock while he moved on to the next place where Christ was still unknown. On the other hand, the apostle James was not a missionary but a pastor; he lived and died in Jerusalem, feeding the flock God had given him, not converting the pagan, Gentile idol worshippers of the outer-empire.

Calling "home" a mission field is like calling a men's Sunday school class a nursery. How so? Because we all used to be babies, and maybe sometimes we still act like babies, but hopefully, we no longer are. Ignoring what the Bible teaches about missions has led congregations to spend vital and highly limited missionary resources on local church ministry outreach rather than on the Great Commission.

Points to Ponder

- A mission field is a place where Christ is predominately or entirely unknown and unnamed. Are there any neighborhoods in your town that may fit that description? What will you do about it?

- If the tithe belongs to the Lord, what should we do with it— what we want or what He wants? What steps can we take to accomplish that?

- What is the quickest, cheapest, easiest way to reach an authentic mission field? Is it by sending one of us to preach to them or helping one of them reach their own people? You decide, then do something to facilitate it.

Why Was Samaria Mentioned in the Great Commission and Not Galilee?

S OMETIMES WE CAN only guess why God does what He does. In the Great Commission's targeted regions, three specific locations are mentioned and then the world's uttermost parts. Jerusalem was a city. Judea was the region in which Jerusalem was located. Samaria was the land of the mix-breed Samaritans, who the Jewish religious leaders despised because they were not fully Hebrew. The Samaritans as a race were considered so detestable that one High Priest made it a crime for a priest to pass through the area or speak to a Samaritan, and if he spent the night there, he could be executed.

In the Great Commission, Jesus skipped from Samaria to *"the uttermost"*—seemingly ignoring Galilee where He grew up, performed most of His miracles, and did much of His teaching. Why? Perhaps He didn't need to. Galilee was the first place He went after His resurrection. Most of the people who saw Him, except for metro Jerusalem, would have been Galileans. They didn't have to hear about the death, burial, and resurrection; they had seen it with their own eyes.

In Scripture, those who follow Christ routinely witnessed to those whom they knew. Cornelius arranged for his entire household to learn about Him. The maniac of Gadara met Christ and witnessed to all his compatriots, and those whom Jesus healed spread His name throughout the regions where they lived. Andrew brought his brother Peter to Jesus, and Philip brought Nathanael. But Samaria was not a place that Jewish converts would typically have friends or relatives. It was a "fly-over" region to devout Jews, so unlike Galilee, Samaria had to be deliberately targeted for evangelism by Christ.

I suspect Christ may have been making the point that in our zeal to reach the world, we should not skip over those who are known by us but remain unfamiliar to us, especially when they are so geographically close to us. How strange that we send more missionaries to Mexico than any other country except Brazil, but we don't evangelize the Mexicans who cut our lawns, build our houses and shop in our stores. Perhaps the lesson to be learned is: in our rush to evangelize the ends of the earth, let's not forget our Samaria.

Points to Ponder

- Sometimes we equate "Jerusalem, Judea, and Samaria" with our hometown, our state, and then the rest of the country. That usage is incorrect because "my Samaria" is likely to be "your Jerusalem." His emphasis was not on distance but on reaching those with ample exposure, limited exposure, and no exposure.

- Examine your missions' giving. Where are you on the map? Are your funds targeting the never reached, the partially reached, or lands already saturated with the gospel?

- Are you sprinkling the world with the gospel as a farmer irrigates his fields, or are you pouring your buckets of the Water of Life on one small plot creating a mudhole? Become a sprinkler—not a busted pipe.

EPISODE 52

Missionaries, Leave the City and Go to the Remote Villages!

I MAKE MUCH to-do about a missionary being a church planter and not just a pastor in a foreign land. I do that because it's biblical, and somebody has to. A missionary should work himself out of a job—not deeper into one. I also believe that a mission field is not a place you happen to feel called to go to or take a youth group to, nor is it necessarily a place with dire needs. Every place has them. A mission field is a people, and perhaps at times, a region inhabited by people, of whom most or none have never yet had any or significant exposure to the gospel. That's biblical. What Americans call missions is typically a location with already established churches. We should accept God's definition and fulfill His Commission.

I have spent a good number of years in Honduras and host Visionary Trips there every summer. But Honduras, as a country, is not a mission field. Thousands of churches have been established there. However, there are also thousands of villages where no preacher has ever entered to preach the gospel. How is that possible? It's simple. Most missionaries perform a pastor's function—not a missionary's, and they tend to congregate in the capital and commercial centers. Life is more comfortable there with the availability of private schools, banks, restaurants, malls, and the Internet. In many countries, more than 90 percent of all the missionaries live within a few miles of each other.

I have been to many villages that had never seen an American; they had no electricity or paved roads, no plumbing or industry. In such villages usually none of the villagers have ever ventured more than a few miles away. They have never seen a TV, a semi-truck, a paved road, a lightbulb, an escalator, or a neon sign. They have never ridden on anything other than a mule or cart. They've never been to a beauty salon or attended a ball game. They've never tasted a Whopper and don't even know what it is. Places like these are sometimes less than an hour from the large cities where most missionaries congregate. Nobody knows these villages are there, though most are on a map. To find them means leaving the city and going into the highways and byways. But isn't that what missions is all about? It's not going where everyone else has already gone, but where no one yet has ventured to go. It's building on no man's foundation—not *every* man's foundation.

Points to Ponder

- Missionaries assemble because they were taught to. They pastor rather than continually plant new churches because they were taught to. Do you think it may be time to re-educate the veterans and better train the next generation? Sharing a copy of this book would be a good starting point.

- How would you find unreached villages? Find a road and drive down it. Find a path and hike it. There will always be someone at the end waiting to hear your message. And they will know of other trails you didn't notice.

- Is it wrong to serve in large cities? No. But why plant a garden in a farmer's cultivated fields when you can find an open field where people are just as hungry?

The Four Places
of the Great Commission

T HE GREAT COMMISSION started, not as a pebble's wave rip-
pling in a still pond, but as a meteorite crashing into the seas,
creating a tsunami of evangelism and turning the world upside down.
At its inauguration on the Day of Pentecost, the Holy Spirit allowed
visitors in Jerusalem to hear about the "marvelous works of God" in
their native languages. These visitors were from at least fifteen ethnic
groups, each speaking their own languages while probably capable of
speaking Greek and Hebrew as well. But to which of His "marvelous
works" were they referring? The blind seeing, the deaf hearing, the
lame walking, or the dead living? They were citing all these and more.
But the greatest of His marvelous works was in fulfilling His promise
of sending a Savior and Redeemer, the Lamb of God. He had been
slain for their sins only weeks earlier after many of them had already
arrived in Jerusalem. And He had risen from the grave and had been
seen by hundreds of witnesses among them.

Before departing to Heaven from Bethany, Jesus told His disciples
to go back to Jerusalem and wait for a sign, and upon seeing it fulfilled,
to go out and evangelize the world. He instructed them to cover the
entire world by naming just four locations:

1. **Jerusalem**, where they were waiting as instructed

WHAT IS A MISSION FIELD?

2. **Judea**, the larger, outlying province where Jerusalem was located

3. **Samaria**, a land of mixed-breed Jews situated between Judea and Galilee

4. **The ends of the earth**, which is everywhere else

Every movement has to start somewhere, and Jerusalem was that place. Some have suggested that within a few months, up to one-third of the city's population may have converted to this new Jewish sect, later called Christianity. They would soon run out of people to evangelize. God knew they would need another target. And that next target was Judea, which was the only region of Israel in that day that had a somewhat dominant Jewish influence while still being predominately Gentile in population.

The third target was Samaria, north of Judea and populated by the Samaritans who were part Jew and part Gentile but were considered by the religious Jews to be a mixed-breed abomination. Converting Samaria would not be difficult; after all, Jesus had begun it through contact with the woman at the well and her neighbors.

The final target was the *"uttermost."* But when leaving Samaria traveling north, you enter Galilee, where Jesus had lived and ministered. Perhaps that is why He skipped Galilee and went to the uttermost. Galilee, to the north, already had a witness, as did the Decapolis to the east. And most of His disciples were from Galilee. These two regions are where Jesus performed most of His miracles, such as freeing the maniac of Gadara, feeding the 5000, and healing the centurion's son. Rather than being mentioned separately, Galilee seems to be included with the rest of the world. That may be because at that time, it was up to 80 percent Gentile. Even today, Galilee is once again part of Israel but heavily populated by Arab Gentiles.

Points to Ponder

• Knowledge alone (how to witness) was not sufficient without the Holy Spirit's power and influence. I was taught "methods," as if they are enough, but the Spirit of God guides us in what to say and convicts the hearts of the hearers.

• Historically, the spread of the gospel in a country always begins with converting one or a few. From there, it spreads from border to border and beyond. Where do you see the gospel beginning to spread today?

• Christ did not have to name specific places; He could have said, "Go everywhere." Why do you suppose He targeted those that He mentioned?

What Missions
Is Not

Episodes 14, 15, 16, 29

Shortcuts and Recognition

A MERICANS TEND TO always look for shortcuts and unearned recognition.

Gone are the days of awarding trophies to those who excel above their peers. Excelling now means merely participating while doing no more or less than anyone else on the team. While growing up, we (and others) could judge our intellect and grasp of a subject by the following letters: A, B, C, D, or F. One letter spoke volumes. Now, all we get is an "acceptable" or "needs improvement."

By what criteria and by whose standards is "acceptable" determined. I don't want an *acceptable* pilot flying me anywhere or an *acceptable* surgeon opening my skull—even if *acceptable* is superior to "needs improvement."

This same mentality of shortcuts to recognition has infiltrated churches as well. Gone are the days when we earned the "missionary" title by personal sacrifice, untiring effort, and ministry accomplishments in lands where our very presence was both evident and perilous. Today we teach our church members that if they give a tract to the waitress at lunch, they are a missionary. Those who make such statements innocently diminish what a missionary is biblically. Is just passing out tracts really what we think missionaries do? Whoever taught you that should go back to school.

Our devoted pastors <u>teach</u> us God's Word, but so do Sunday school teachers. They both teach, but there is a difference in being a pastor and being a Sunday school teacher. If we have taught that being a missionary is so simple and the job requirements so easily attained, is it any wonder why raising missionary support is so difficult? And why would we expect our young people to be interested in doing throughout their adult life what they already did as a child?

Truthfully, we dishonor the missionary's calling and minimize its importance if the requirements can be so easily attained. Missions is not the Little League; it's the Major League, and church, it's time to "play ball."

Points to Ponder

- How would you define a missionary? What does he do and not do?

- Jeremiah wrote that we should not "seek great things for ourselves," yet most of us want to be great. Better to be what God made you and let Him assign the greatness. You are not great because of what you accomplish; you are great because you accomplish what God intended for you.

- Read missionary biographies and see how they failed at their intentions but triumphed at God's.

Missions Is Not Social Work, but Should Include It

S OCIAL WORK IS not missions, but a wise missionary will use social work to expose the gospel further, allowing the lost to "see
our good works and glorify our Father," as Matthew 5:16 teaches. Some
fear that giving away band-aids and porridge will eventually snuff out
the preaching of the gospel. They are right in many cases, but they
don't have to be. Simply because some people put the cart before the
horse doesn't mean everyone has to—or will.

Jesus frequently healed and fed the needy and even raised Lazarus
from the dead. Tabitha's testimony was that she clothed the widows.
George Mueller cared for over 10,000 orphans in his lifetime, and William Carey started the first primary and girl's school in India, a Bible
college, and India's first degree-offering university. He also started the
first Bengali newspaper and the India Horticultural Society. He used
every social opportunity possible in a meaningful way to spread the
gospel throughout India. Yet, despite all his many and massive social
programs, he is still revered in India and worldwide as a missionary.

Missionaries see social work as a means of obeying Christ's command to feed the hungry, clothe the naked, and care for widows and
orphans. Such programs are not only social but scriptural.

Today, some of the best-known charities no longer preach the gospel. They failed in their calling because they chose to—not because it is inevitable. We, too, can choose to fail or to remain faithful to our primary calling. Demas chose to forsake Paul, but of his entire entourage of more than 70 known disciples, only Demas made that decision; all the others remained faithful. And Paul never avoided future ministry in cities because Demas had chosen their enticement over ministry hardships.

Feeding a hungry family the bread they need to live can open their hearts to accept the Bread of Life. Giving a cup of water in Jesus' name will earn you a heavenly reward and also give the recipient a chance to hear how they can drink and never thirst again.

Points to Ponder

- Because others have failed in using social efforts to spread the gospel does not mean we should not use them. Or does it? What do you think?

- What social works could you perform in your community that would let "your light shine?"

- Should missionary training include "how-to" instructions using social work as a tool to enhance their ministry?

- Would you like to join me on a Visionary Trip and help socially while you minister spiritually? If so, give me a call.

EPISODE 16

Missions Travel Has Changed

MISSIONS TRAVEL HAS changed. Today you can fly from England to India in less than half a day, but two hundred years ago, it took months of sailing through some of the most treacherous and pirate-infested waters in the world. And if the waves didn't get you, the heat, rotting food, and onboard diseases could. Travel was so dangerous that many died on their journey before reaching their field. For example, David Livingstone's wife and child died along the Zambezi River before ever arriving at their destination.

Scottish missionary John Payton, whose family traveled to the New Hebrides Islands in the South Pacific, lost his first wife and newborn son only three months after arriving. Because of the island culture, he had to sleep on his wife and children's graves until they had decomposed to prevent the cannibals from digging up their bodies to eat them. When he died, the islanders, having been converted, inscribed his memorial saying, "When John Peyton arrived there were no Christians; when he died, there were no cannibals."

The purpose of traveling is to survive getting to the place where men need to hear the gospel. Whatever your effort—crossing the piranha-infested Amazon, or enduring altitude sickness in the Andes, or wading through swamps in an Asian delta, or being so deep in an African jungle that you cannot use the sun to judge your direction—

the dangers along the trail are not what matters; it is the prize at the end of the trail.

In his travels, Paul shared that he had been beaten with a rod, received some 200 lashes, left for death, stoned, imprisoned multiple times, shipwrecked three times, and for many years, suffered hunger, nakedness, cold, and sickness. We know that at least once he survived being bitten by a poisonous snake. What a journey! What a prize! What a crown!

Missionary travel has changed, but our message has not, and it yet remains for the entire world to hear at least once what we have heard all our lives. Our task is not yet complete. Put on your traveling shoes and get out there.

Points to Ponder

- We all like to complain, but we should compare the trials of our travel with those who have gone before us. My darling wife always refers to our travels as "adventures." That attitude makes them both bearable and enjoyable.

- When reading missionary biographies, please pay attention to what they had to endure and how thankful they were to be "counted worthy" to suffer for Christ.

- Some people enjoy strange food, strange lands, and strange customs. If you are one of them, what is it about your outlook that makes the difference?

- What is the strangest thing you ever ate?

Missions Is Not Church Work; It's Church Planting

IN THE 1700S, MISSIONARIES were church planters in other cultures. Generally, these other cultures were in foreign lands with foreign customs, foods, lifestyles, and languages. Sometimes, like in the Americas, the cultures were totally different but not so far away. They were often less than a day's walk into the forest. Such missionary endeavors to the American Indians were carried out in the northeast by missionaries like David Brainerd and in the southeast by missionaries like John Wesley.

As they ventured farther into the forests, they left behind small tribal churches that were sometimes led by tribal preachers and sometimes by other foreigners. Usually, their efforts produced congregations that developed needed ministries like schools and orphanages. Ministers—not missionaries—first staffed such worthwhile ministries. In time, the staff of specialized workers such as doctors and teachers would outgrow the church-planting missionaries. Because of this and the need for these workers to be supported, it did not take long before the term *missionary* had morphed from being church planters to becoming merely church workers. From there, the term *missionary* took another hit to its original definition, in that missionaries almost ceased to be church planters and became virtually, without exception, church pastors and workers.

Today, statistically, most missionaries will never plant a church. They will serve only as a helper or assistant pastor until the aging missionary retires or moves on, then they will take his place. For this reason, most of the dedicated people today who claim to be and are supported as missionaries are only pastors or workers.

There are two missionary misconceptions prevalent today:

1) All missionaries are church planters. This conception is factually incorrect.

2) A missionary doesn't have to be a church planter. This understanding is biblically incorrect.

To fulfill the Great Commission, pastors need to re-educate our churches that a missionary is not a church *worker*; he is a church *planter*.

Points to Ponder

- Do you see the distinction between church work and missionary work? How would you illustrate the difference?

- Do you understand that a missionary is a starter, and pastors and laypeople are the finishers?

- What do you feel are the dangers in redefining missionaries from being a church planter and discipler of church planters and performing other functions currently ascribed to missionaries, i.e., children's workers, teachers, pilots, pastors, etc.?

What Is a
Biblical Missionary?

Episodes 7, 8, 9, 10, 11, 30, 33, 34, 47, 48, 51

Misunderstandings About What a Missionary Is Part 1 — Purpose

I**N EPHESIANS 4, GOD** reveals five gifts designed to bring us from conversion to spiritual maturity and perpetuate the church until His return. These gifts are apostles, prophets, evangelists, pastors, and teachers. The word *apostle* is the Greek word from which we derive the word *missionary*. He lays the foundation that the others will build upon. The other four gifts are ministers.

1. A *prophet* is an exhorter of the Word—not a mystic fortune teller.

2. An *evangelist* evangelizes, i.e., wins the lost as naturally as a pastor leads the flock. They are not traveling preachers who minister in churches. (Philip the evangelist had two daughters; the Bible also called them "evangelists.")

3. The final two positions—*pastor* and *teacher*—are well understood, and thus, are self-explanatory.

The missionary is called and equipped by God to be the first messenger to enter a culture or region. His job is to proclaim Christ and establish a beachhead from which other ministers will both expand in outreach and mature the new converts. He declares the message that the true God does not take; He gives. He does not destroy; He restores. He does not hate; He loves. He is not a man who became a god; He is the God who became a man. He does not demand a sacrifice; He became our sacrifice. He did not live then die; He lived, died, and now lives again. Such a message has never been heard nor imagined—until the missionary comes. He paves the way for the future ministers who will follow him. Their combined efforts will produce more missionaries, preachers, evangelists, pastors, teachers, and so on in perpetuity.

Today, many want to get paid for ministry and often call themselves a "missionary" to get support. There are even self-proclaimed missionary plumbers and missionaries to the fashion industry. Such titles are absurd and unbiblical. These industries do not require missionaries but rather a faithful witness from local church members. It's not what you call yourself that makes you a missionary; it's what you do. Understanding the real, biblical purpose of a missionary is key to fulfilling the Great Commission.

Points to Ponder

- Modern Christianity has changed the definition of *missionary*, so too have we changed the definition of *evangelist*. In doing this, we ignore that God chooses women as witnesses too. How do you think that has affected the spread of Christianity? (I address this issue at great length in my book, *Great Commission Conundrums*.)

- Consider that a missionary's purpose is to lay the foundation of Christianity in a previously unreached place. Without him doing so, there is no church. You must pour the foundation before the structure can be built. Shouldn't that cause us to honor the position rather than ignore it, relegating it to a lower position?

- Regarding sending more and more "missionaries" to the same place, just how many foundations do you need to pour before you start building?

Misunderstandings About What a Missionary Is Part 2 — Duration

From childhood, I was taught (by their example) that missionaries go to a single foreign field and stay there forever. I've heard of missionaries who lost their support because they moved from one country to another. Some pastors feel that a missionary's moving from one place to another demonstrates that he does not know God's will. Yet many pastors move from church to church, following God's will. The book of Acts reveals that Paul didn't go to only one place; he went to many. He stayed in Thessalonica for only three weeks, and Corinth, his most prolonged stay in any one place, hosted him for several years.

It is not how long you stay that makes you a missionary. At least three biblical criteria make that determination:

1. **Where you go** (Who are the people you go to reach?)

2. **What you do** (Do you plant churches and train church planters or pastor a single congregation?)

3. **Why you leave** (Is it to go elsewhere and repeat the process or to abandon your calling for another?)

It all comes down to one simple question: What is the difference between a missionary and a traveling preacher or pastor? Here's the answer: missions is the intentional relocating of your ministry from the regions informed about the gospel to another uninformed region. It is about exposing the unexposed to the gospel—nothing more, nothing less, nothing else. Pastoring is about maturing the converts. The traveling preacher (prophet) is an exhorter, assisting pastors with their teachings. An evangelist evangelizes-outside the church facility—not inside where believers gather.

Paul once announced that he was moving from Corinth to Spain. His stated reason was that where he and his disciples had been serving in the regions of Galatia and Achaia, there was no place left for him to preach. Surely, some towns and churches would have been eager and honored to host Paul. What he meant was that since he was not a pastor but a missionary ordained by God to take the gospel to those regions without exposure to it, he had no choice but to relocate to find another uninformed, unevangelized region and start again. Thus, he was moving to Spain. Biblically, pastors *move* to an established area to feed the sheep, while missionaries *move on* and plant new churches.

Points to Ponder

- Considering the biblical example of Paul, do you feel a missionary must go to one town or country and stay there his entire life?

- Do you see how God's ministerial gifts to the church are strategically designed to enter an unreached place and birth, mature, multiply, perpetuate and expand the church there and beyond?

- How has the modern-day relocation of these gifts affected His plan?

Misunderstandings
About What a Missionary Is
Part 3 — Language

A T AGE 11, I felt a call to missions. From that point on, I lis-
tened to and learned from every missionary I met. I became
convinced that I had to learn another language to be a missionary
merely by their examples. Hence, as I grew older, I naturally wondered
why missionaries served in England, Australia, Belize, and other English-speaking countries. I was a bit confused.

As I began to study the Bible, I couldn't find any place where Paul
preached to Gentiles in any language other than Greek—a language as
familiar to Paul as English is to me. As I studied his ministry methods,
I began to see a pattern emerge. Paul never had to attend language
school. His emphasis was on penetrating cities that were the cultural
seats of a surrounding region. Each community was distinguished
by its primary or patron god or goddess. These may have also been
known and worshipped in other regions, but they were secondary
to the region's primary deity. Corinth primarily worshipped Apollo,
Ephesus worshipped Diana, Athens, of course, worshipped Athena.
When Paul and Barnabas first began to perform miracles and evangelize in Lystra, Timothy's hometown, the citizens believed them to be
Jupiter and Mercury.

Besides each region having its own regional god, they also had their own regional language—just as Paul had his native language of Hebrew. Through military occupation, languages often died, but even when a local language survived, the people typically were forced to speak the Empire's language. Statistically today, a language dies every two weeks, and 96 percent of the world speaks one of four languages.

So then, it's not the languages you speak that make you a missionary; it's the message you proclaim. Missionaries don't always have to be bilingual if English is well known locally or if they have an interpreter.

And for the record, at this writing there are 225 million English speakers in America, but there are 220 million English speakers in India and Pakistan.

Points to Ponder

- English is the official language of 67 countries and 27 other territories. It is the most spoken language in the world, barely surpassing Mandarin Chinese. The impact is primarily due to the British Empire's former expansion and the USA's leadership worldwide.

- Had you ever considered that Paul never had to go to a language school?

- What languages do you speak? Most people enjoy listening to someone who attempts to communicate with them. They are tickled by our errors and honored that we are making an effort. Swallow your pride and try to talk to foreigners you meet in your town. Your attempts could lead to their salvation.

Misunderstandings About What a Missionary Is Part 4 — Location

I GREW UP thinking that a missionary goes from point A to point B to witness, but I was wrong. As far as we know, Peter, James, Philip, and Stephen never left the Roman Empire's boundaries. They ministered as pastors, evangelists, and deacons, but Paul was a missionary. They all served in the same empire preaching the same gospel.

So why did they have different titles? Quite simply, they had different purposes. Those men mentioned preached where people knew of Christ to one degree or another, but Paul preached where Christ was unknown—until he arrived. The seats of Christianity—Jerusalem, Damascus, Alexandria, and Antioch all had the gospel, but Thessalonica, Athens, and Berea did not. The citizens were all living under Roman rule; they all spoke Greek, shared commerce and education, but had a different level of exposure to the gospel.

Some Americans who minister overseas are called "missionaries." National preachers minister alongside of them in the same church, but they are called "pastors"—same message, same location, same people, but a different title. Why? In my younger church planting work in New York City, I learned if I pastored in upstate New York, I would be called a "pastor," but because I was planting a church in the New York City area, I was called a "missionary." Yet, there was and is no Scripture to support that thinking.

A place does not qualify as a mission field because it is far from home or has a different language or culture. It is a mission field because there is an absence of the preaching of the gospel, and the inhabitants know little or nothing of Christ. It's all about access.

If the gospel is there and available without restriction, then it is not a *mission* field; it is a *ministry* field. Those needed to preach and serve in regions where Christ is known are not missionaries but evangelists, pastors, deacons, and laypeople. If there really is no purpose in these different callings of God, then why go elsewhere when we can stay home and do the same thing?

Points to Ponder

● Do you see that you are not a missionary because of where you go, but *why* you go? If your purpose is to shepherd a congregation, you are not doing missionary work; you are pastoring.

● How many missionaries were taught otherwise? Could that be a huge reason why we have not fulfilled the Great Commission?

● Nothing is wrong with starting a new church in an area that already has them; God leads where God leads. But was it biblically correct for me to be called a "missionary" while planting a church minutes north of New York City—in a place that already had scores of churches already established for centuries?

Misunderstandings
About What a Missionary Is
Part 5 — Culture

IN MY YOUTH, I thought a missionary looked like me but went to preach to people who did not look like me, dress like me or even eat like me. They were different.

This misunderstanding has led many missionary families to return home. In fact, over half the missionaries who make it to the foreign field don't last beyond their first term. All the years of deputation and language study were for nothing. When questioned, the primary reason given for not returning was their inability to adapt to the culture.

Missionaries, justified or not, have universally gained the reputation that we try to change the culture of the people we go to reach. After bringing them to Christ we often unintentionally try to turn them into American Christians, teaching them to wear suits and ties to church when their own President doesn't even dress that way. Our example influences their clothing styles, musical preferences, eating habits, and ministry schedules. National churches are happy to meet in a house or under a tree until they learn that American churches have buildings with steeples. They are not distracted by babies crying, roosters crowing, or even the occasional dog sleeping at the pastor's feet—until we teach them they are supposed to be distracted by those things and make arrangements to prevent them.

WHAT IS A BIBLICAL MISSIONARY?

When I believed that a missionary was someone like me who went to preach to those who were not like me, I was wrong. In our failure to reach them, the problem is not that they are not like us, but that we are not like them. Paul emphasized this when he said, *"I am made all things to all men, that I might by all means save some. And this I do for the gospel's sake, that I might be partaker thereof with you"* (I Corinthians 9:22b-23). In other words, Paul said, "I never tried to make you like me; I became like you so that I might become one of you and bring you to Christ." We, as missionaries, should not have to *endure* other cultures; we should *assimilate* them.

Points to Ponder

- Imagine if your pastor was from an Asian tribe. He only wore his tribal clothing (a modest, mini-skirt-length tunic). He always ate his traditional food (grub worms and roasted dog). He only allowed his preference of musical instruments (bamboo flutes and drums) and insisted everyone sit on the floor. How effective would his ministry be? How enticing would it be for your neighbors to join your church?

- When we force our cultural preferences on other societies, those who do convert are often seen as traitors to their own people, desiring to be like foreigners rather than their forefathers. This change diminishes the strength of their witness.

- What do you think Paul meant by becoming one of them? Consider that he had to do that everywhere he went. I wonder if he experienced culture shock. Assimilation exterminates culture shock.

Titles Have Consequences

THE BIBLE EMPHASIZES, by example, that a missionary is a church planter. He may wear a pastor's hat for a short time while training others, but his calling is to plant churches. In Ephesians 4, Scripture makes a distinction between being a pastor and being a missionary. Shouldn't we make that distinction as well? If every jot and tittle is important, then the tittles God chose to use are important as well; and we should not alter, ignore or redefine them.

For example, in the 1980s, American churches grew accustomed to giving any religious worker living overseas the title of *missionary*. This tradition continued, and as a result, the majority of those serving as "missionaries" today are actually teachers, orphanage workers, or church staff.

The 1990s brought more changes to the definition of the title *missionary*. Others, also needing to raise support for their ministries here in America, changed their title from *evangelist* to "missionary." Now we have missionary carpenters, missionary prison chaplains, missionaries to military bases, and even missionary plumbers. The truth is, every missionary should evangelize, but every person who does so is not necessarily a missionary.

"So, what's the problem?" you may ask. "After all, it's just a title."

Here's the problem, when you change the definition of a term, you also change its purpose. That is why today, most missionaries have never started a church. They serve only in ministry functions and don't even realize they are not fulfilling the purpose of the calling they claim to have. Quite simply, if you are not a church planter, you are not a missionary, though you may be a minister of the gospel. Both could and should be supported. So, support missionaries as missionaries, and support workers, pastors, teachers, etc., as worthy ministers of the gospel. Don't rob Paul to pay Peter.

A church may have many teachers and preachers, but only one is called pastor. A hospital may have scores of health-care professionals, but only the qualified are called doctors. Even airlines have thousands of employees, but only the tested and experienced few are called pilots. If titles aren't important, then why, Dad, Mom, do you have one?

Points to Ponder

- Name ten titles, i.e., doctor, lawyer, whose meanings are apparent.

- Can you name one that is not?

- Do you now see how important a title can be and how redefining it can changes the word and, in time, the world?

- How can we restore the original meaning of what it means to be a missionary?

Some Missionaries Start Poorly but End Well

S OME START WELL and end poorly in missionary work, like Demas. Others start poorly but end well, like John Mark.

John Mark was the son of Mary, in whose home the early church in Jerusalem met, and he was also related to Peter and Barnabas, Paul's first missionary partner. Barnabas and Paul took Mark with them as their assistant and *protégé* on their first journey to Barnabas' homeland of Cyprus (Acts 13:5). However, at the second stop on their journey in Perga, John Mark, for some reason, abandoned the team and went home.

Sometime later, after Paul met with the Council in Jerusalem, Barnabas suggested they allow Mark to join them again. He wanted to give his nephew a second chance. Despite his admiration for his superior Barnabas, Paul was so adamantly opposed that he and Barnabas parted ways, never to minister together again. This denouncement would have discouraged most men beyond repair, but not Mark. Whatever had persuaded him to abandon the team years earlier had been cast aside and was no longer a weight to deter him from running his race.

Even before Paul's conversion, John Mark had been with Jesus often and even on the night of His arrest. And now, within a decade of Paul's rejection, Mark had gained experience under the tutelage of both Barnabas and possibly Peter, another relative, and once again, had evidently served for some time with Paul as well (Colossians 4:10). Years later, according to tradition, he would serve as a translator for Peter in Rome, start the church in Alexandria, became its first bishop, and wrote Mark's gospel.

A few years after Paul's rejection of John Mark, he wrote to the church at Colossae and told them to welcome Mark, and then as Paul awaited his execution in Rome, he sat to write his last letter—II Timothy. He told Timothy that Demas, who had started well, had now forsaken him and that only doctor Luke was with him. He asked Timothy to come to visit; bring him his books to read, his parchments to study, his winter coat; and bring John Mark with him because "he is profitable to me for the ministry." Paul, who once refused to train or even work with him, now chose John Mark as his final ministry partner. At the end of his life, he did not call on any of the men he had personally trained or nurtured, but on the one Barnabas had patiently discipled, who started poorly and ended well.

Points to Ponder

- Our churches have lost many men because we did not have the patience to deal with them. Do you know of any such men? I do. What can we do to reclaim them?

- Some have said, "The church is the only army on earth that shoots its wounded." Is that a good testimony for us to have?

- When a pastor/preacher/dedicated worker falls due to lust, should we abandon him forever as being useless to God and man, or should we "restore such a one in the spirit of meekness, considering ourselves, lest we also be tempted" (Galatians 6:1)? Can you start on that today?

Some Missionaries Start Well but End Poorly

A S I STATED in the previous lesson, in any calling some start well and end poorly, and others start poorly and end well. The Bible gives two missionary examples of this dichotomy in Demas and John Mark, who I addressed in the last lesson.

Demas was with Paul and Epaphras during Paul's first imprisonment in Rome. He was evidently a fellow prisoner who had chosen to suffer with the apostle rather than enjoy the world's pleasures. Some speculate that Demas was from the church in Thessalonica and left Paul to return home, but no one knows for sure.

What is known is that Demas was among the chosen few of Paul's converts or disciples considered approved and eligible to travel with and minister to the apostle. There had to have been something in his manner, character, devotion, or potential which would cause Paul to invite him to be a team member. There is every reason to believe that for a time, Demas succeeded. After all, unlike John Mark, Paul never sent Demas away, and Paul had at least once called him a "fellow laborer"—which was a way of saying Paul considered him to be his coworker and confidant.

Earlier, he had been with Paul or sent by Paul to serve with Luke and Epaphras in Colossae. But now, at the time of Paul's impending death, he stated that Demas had forsaken him. The word he used means "to abandon" or "to leave helpless." Polycarp later taught that Demas had abandoned Paul in Rome shortly before his execution. So it appears he stayed near to the end, but not to the end.

Perhaps he desired the security of life over death. Perhaps comfort was more appealing than suffering. Perhaps his sense of confidence was not in Christ but Paul. Even today, many abandon their service for Christ when their spiritual leader dies or succumbs to sin. We don't know his reason, but we can learn from his example. Today, 55 percent of the missionaries who make it past their first four years never return to the field. Their primary reason for forsaking the field is their inability to adapt to the foreign culture. Like Demas, they started well and ended poorly. John Mark, however, started poorly and ended well. Would to God we could all start well and end well.

Points to Ponder

- *"For Demas hath forsaken me..."* is the declaration that followed him into eternity. Even with all the successes he had, he is known for the failure. There is no historical record of him returning to service. He loved, but not the Lord, not Paul and his companions, and not the ministry. He loved the world. We don't know what redirected his love, but we can learn from it and beware of the influence of anything that takes our eyes off the Lord. Where our eyes go, our hearts follow. "Oh, be careful little eyes what you see...."

- Do you think if Demas had a chance to do it over, he would do it differently? What would you do differently? Think about that for a moment privately, then put those things behind and move forward for Christ.

The Biblical Missionary vs.
Our Modern Viewpoint

W E LIKE TO think that what we do is biblical—but it may
not be. However, saying something is not biblical doesn't
mean it's wrong or sinful; it only means that there is no mention of it
in Scripture. For example, there is no biblical reference to a church
building. The first one wasn't built until the mid-third century. Nor is
there any mention of a bus ministry, a youth pastor, or a mission conference, but that does not mean they are wrong. All are logical, useful,
and facilitate doing what God called us to do.

There are other things, though not sinful, that can lead us to detract from or even forget what we do have a biblical basis for doing. For
example, the early church used their tithes to support their pastors and
missionaries and care for the needy and afflicted. Today, the majority
of our tithes pay the mortgage and cover the maintenance needs of
our buildings. That's not a sin; we need buildings to hold our growing
congregation and shield us from rain, sleet, snow, and heat; but they
can detract from the purpose God gave for the tithe.

Most churches spend far more on their facilities than they do on
missions. And many American pastors don't even receive a salary
because the tithe is consumed on other things. Thank God the early
church understood the biblical purpose of the tithe, and because of

this understanding, they *"turned the world upside down"* (Acts 17:6). What have we done lately?

Truthfully, if we didn't have a building with heat and AC, many of our most faithful members would not attend. Those who justify the American house church movement because "church buildings are not biblical" should remember that the early church members did not drive cars to their house churches either. They had no central heat and air, no recorded music to sing with, or any other trinkets that typify an American concept of what a church is. They didn't even have membership forms.

Regarding missions, we think it's simply sending some of us to some of them, moving preachers like chess-pieces from point A to point B. We expect the missionary to go, oversee an established church or maybe start one, which statistically is extremely rare, and then remain there (which is less than a 6-percent probability) until he retires or dies. Then his board will replace him with yet another one of us. Where do you find that model in the Bible?

Points to Ponder

- Do you understand the difference between non-biblical (no scriptural example or mention) and unbiblical (contrary to scriptural teaching)?

- Is it non-biblical or unbiblical for a missionary not to be a church planter?

- Some contend it is unbiblical to support national missionaries instead of Americans. Can you think of even one verse that states or implies that teaching? If not, then it is unbiblical to say, "It is unbiblical to support national missionaries."

Principles of
Paul's Missionary Example

W E DON'T KNOW how many missionary trips Paul had taken or everywhere he went. The Bible tells us about only three of his trips, and from these, we can see a pattern emerge.

1] **Paul went to strategic, cultural centers.** From there the gospel could flow downstream, as did their commerce, governmental authority, and pagan faith.

2] **Paul never pastored a church long-term that we know of, though he did teach and preach.** He assigned pastors from among those who traveled with him, like Timothy and Titus, or he appointed them from among the new converts, like Tychicus and Erastus. But Paul never solicited help from a Jewish replacement. He knew the best person to reach the Greek was another Greek.

3] **Paul never stayed anywhere long.** In Thessalonica, he stayed less than three weeks, but in that short time, he planted a church, appointed a leader, and then moved on. Why? Because biblically, a missionary is not a pastor in a foreign country; he is a church planter, going wherever the gospel is yet to be preached.

4] **Paul had a home base.** He spent a great deal of time in Antioch between trips, serving in his home church and in Jerusalem, meeting with the brethren, and being obedient to his Judaic traditions. He also visited the churches he and his disciples had started, encouraging the believers and correcting any doctrinal and lifestyle errors. And then, of course, there were his years in prison, where he wrote his letters.

5] **Paul never considered a place to be an "uttermost part of the earth" after planting a church there.** It was now a "Jerusalem" to be fully evangelized by the local church. He then moved on to turn more "uttermost" areas into more "Jerusalems."

Finally, from Paul's example, we learn that you are not a missionary because of where you live or how long you live there. You are a missionary because of what you do and where you do it. If you are a Pauline missionary, you are, first and foremost and forever, both a church planter and a discipler of church planters.

Points to Ponder

- How many missionaries do you know who plant multiple churches and train multiple men to do so?

- It is taught that Paul always went to large cities, but the Bible proves otherwise. Philippi was a small town of about 2,000 people, mostly immigrants.

- Of the 44 places Paul visited, most were coastal, excluding Jerusalem (not a missionary visit), Damascus (while in training), four in Galatia (Iconium, Derbe, Lystra, and Antioch), and Berea, which was fewer than twenty miles inland. Thirty-seven of the forty-four were seaports. Perhaps being along trade routes and having accessibility to rapid flight played a more significant role than population.

Nuggets of Missionary Gold—
Become One of Them

MANY VERSES IN the New Testament give us insight and understanding of missions and a missionary's work. Once discovered and assimilated, these verses will change the missionary's life forever. One addresses the concept of our becoming "one of them."

The approach sounds simple, yet most missionaries are never taught it, and therefore, never discover it. We are, in fact, taught to do exactly the opposite—teach them to become like us. For example, travel to any developing nation, and you will see the western steeples of church buildings piercing the local landscape. We teach them to wear white shirts and ties to be respectful to God. We give them nicknames from our culture, feed them our food, and expect them to wear our clothing.

Missionary Hudson Taylor realized that exporting his British culture to China along with the gospel message hindered some Chinese from accepting Christ. Many thought that becoming a Christian meant to become British and adapt their food, clothing, and lifestyle. In response, he moved out of the mission compound to a rented room. He wore the clothes of a Chinese coolie, the lower class of the people, and grew his hair long for a queue, the ponytail worn by Chinamen. Though he may or may not have known, the queue had a religious significance in their culture.

Taylor was such an embarrassment to his fellow missionaries and board that they disowned him. Being alone and without funds, he started the China Inland Mission. He revolutionized missions by taking the gospel from the seacoast to inland China, an area intentionally overlooked by the missionaries. Doing this, he began a new age of missions and a pattern that missionaries copied worldwide.

Taylor was not the first to discover new insights into missions. You were likely taught that Paul's name was changed from *Saul* to Paul on the road to Damascus. The name change happened years later—on his first missionary trip to the Gentiles to whom God called him. He abandoned his Hebrew name *Saul* for the Roman equivalent, Paul. He intentionally identified with them even in his persona. Identifying with the people was his first step in becoming "all things to all men, that by all means, he might save some." And even before Paul, the greatest missionary, Jesus, became one of us so we could understand His message.

Points to Ponder

- Would you be willing to adopt a new lifestyle, food, clothing, etc., to be accepted and produce fruit for Christ?

- Early single British missionaries to Africa, whose message would not be accepted because of coming from foreigners, married African women to "become one of them." It worked.

- Western culture is global, so there is less for us to change unless you target unreached tribal groups. Can you find some online to pray for and support national missionaries to reach them? They live in their backyards.

Starting Churches, the Result of Missions

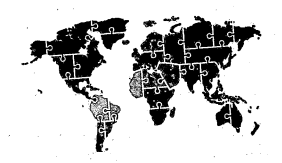

Episodes 19, 23, 25, 31

Birthing New Churches

G IVING BIRTH IS a dual experience of trauma and triumph. Many women giving birth to their first child find the event painful, but by the third, fourth or fifth child, some testify that the experience passed virtually unnoticed. No matter the pain of giving birth, we cherish the loving relationship that led to that moment.

Birthing churches is comparable. Some lament the pains and strains involved in birthing a new church. Others view it as a joyful experience for the missionary, whose labors brought forth the new congregation. Paul birthed new churches everywhere he went and expected his disciples to do likewise. For him, the birthing process was natural—enter a town, convert the lost, collect the converts into a congregation, then disciple them to reasonable maturity so that they can do likewise.

Many missionaries will never start a new church. They view the task as something to be avoided. Others make the mistake of transporting new converts to their services from miles away for the sake of numbers, rather than birthing a new congregation in their area. Still, others are hindered, when yielding to the distraction of unnecessary details, including whether there is enough money; enough workers; an available building; and available funds for seats, signs, and songbooks. These concerns prevent us from bringing new converts together to fellowship, pray, study, and encourage one another. Truthfully, if we worried as much about the logistics of birthing a new baby as we do of birthing a new church, New York City would be known as New York Village. Paul's method was to plant new congregations in the homes of new converts so that from there, they could be the church in their community. He had no start-up costs.

Starting a new church should be as natural as adding a new family member. Where there is love, the reality of a pregnancy is always a blessing. Any sacrifice made for the benefit of the new child is gladly accepted. Likewise, birthing a new church should bring joy, regardless of sacrifices that the parent-missionary team or congregation must accept to benefit the new-born church. God wants the entire world to be filled with the knowledge of His glory. His method to accomplish this is by expanding His family into every community through the birthing of new churches.

Points to Ponder

- A family does not grow by dividing one child into two; God's plan is multiplication, not division. The same is true for birthing new churches. A church split is not a new church; rather, it is the continuation of a single, divided congregation that could not or would not reconcile.

- New babies are conceived without announcement, anticipation, or knowledge. So too, new churches are often birthed without intention or expectation. One convert, being discipled, attracts others and soon, you have a congregation (church). It doesn't take nine months.

- Have you ever been involved in birthing a new church? Billions of babies have been born at *home* until "civilization" determined we could do it better in a hospital. So too, missionaries started most churches *in a home* until we were taught it is better to have a more planned, organized, sterile environment for the birth. The Western method prepares for the baby in advance of the birth, waiting for its arrival. The biblical example accepts the baby when and where it is born and then nurtures it with whatever it needs. Typically, all it needs for a while is nourishment from the one who birthed it.

Birthing Churches,
Then Letting Them Go

W E OFTEN TALK about birthing new churches, but what about maturing them? Some consider national pastors as being ignorant compared to the "educated" Westerner, but they have not had Christianity for thousands of years to guide and affect their culture. Nor have they had schools of higher learning to drown their zeal in deep pools of theological debates. Globally, many pastors and most Christians don't even own a Bible, but they do know how to love.

The missionary's responsibility is to found the church, whether he be an American or a national. The missionary's duty is also to provide a qualified pastor to shepherd the new congregation. It is not his duty or his right to perpetually keep these new congregations under his control. Shepherding is like parenting. We guide and teach our children while they are ignorant, immature, and inexperienced. As they mature, our methods and context of raising them change. We shouldn't expect them to remain under our control all their lives. If they do, our parenting has failed. Either we did not know how to parent effectively, or our need to be needed led us to handicap their maturity intentionally.

Over the centuries, and even today, many national churches go from loving the missionary and depending on him for everything to resenting him because he will not let them go, grow and lead their own churches.

Conquerors maintain perpetual and forceful control; shepherds guide with love and patience. If we must remain in charge because, allegedly, we cannot trust the nationals, we diminish the Holy Spirit's work and insult our own accomplishments. Maturity should come over time and with it, authority. Consider that Paul left every church he started, but he left national pastors to guide them. The instructions he gave later, i.e., correcting doctrinal error and encouraging godly behavior, were given from a distance and communicated to them via the letters he sent through their pastors. If a church needs correction, better it should be due to their ignorance than our arrogance.

Points to Ponder

- As a mother provides her infant's only nourishment, the missionary will do the same for the infant church for a short time. In moving on, he does not abandon the toddling congregation; instead, he appoints others to care for the growing church. They are the maturing gifts God mentions in Ephesian chapter four. Prophets (preachers), evangelists to grow the congregation, pastors to shepherd it, and teachers.

- Every couple wants their baby to mature physically, emotionally, spiritually, and mentally. So too is our desire for newborn churches. One parent cannot do it all; it takes a mother, father, grandparents, siblings, etc. The missionary may give birth to the church; that is his job, but if he does not allow the others to do theirs, the infant will remain an infant. And the missionary will fail to produce more babies.

Immediate Evangelism
Upon Salvation

S OME TEACH THAT spiritual maturity should precede evangelism and church planting; they teach that a new congregation
should not start other churches until they are mature in the faith. The
question is, at what point are any of us fully matured? The New Testament speaks of our coming to spiritual maturity only when we are
finally in the presence of God. For now, any step along that journey is
just that—a step—not an arrival.

Others believe that when a person accepts Christ, he is capable
and should share his conversion with friends, family, and even strangers in the hope of bringing them to Christ. He is not bringing them to
spiritual maturity, but to a full, saving faith in Christ alone—no longer
reliant on their former gods, idols, or good works. Andrew, upon his
conversion, immediately sought his brother Simon Peter and brought
him to Christ.

The first group believes you cannot witness and plant churches until you know all there is to know. The second group believes that a seed
planted in fertile soil will grow and produce fruit, whether planted by
an agriculturalist with a PhD or an illiterate dirt-farmer. A seed in the
soil is a seed in the soil.

The commission of Christ is to cover the earth with the knowledge of His glory. This spiritual seed, when dispersed, will bring forth fruit, more fruit, much fruit and fruit that remains, as the Lord requested in His prayer. The idea that we must leave evangelizing and church planting to an educated and ordained few has for centuries hampered the spread of Christianity.

Though educated and ordained, Paul was a tentmaker by profession, a man who persecuted Christians and would have been among those who condemned Christ. But after conversion, he immediately and continually preached in Damascus and was greatly responsible for the spontaneous growth of Christianity.

James, John, Peter, Matthew, and all the others who had lived with Christ for years personally witnessed all He did and heard all He taught, yet were nonetheless happy, for a time, to remain at home rather than go into all the world as commanded. Perhaps living in a city with thousands of Christians, they still saw Jerusalem as "their" *mission* field rather than as a *ministry* field. Thank God Paul was not among them. Are we?

Points to Ponder

● Witnessing is the natural expression of our faith for which we are so grateful and so delighted that we cannot keep silent. Dads, have you ever told your child, "I love you, and Mommy loves you too"? You were a witness of her love for them. Being a witness of God's love for the world is no more complicated than that.

● As Americans, we often birth new churches by enticing converts to move from one crib to another. *That's kidnapping!* God's way to birth new churches is by producing new babies; we call that *evangelizing* and assembling the new converts into a new nursery.

What Is Church Planting?

I BELIEVE THAT a missionary is, or at least should be, a church planter. But some are confused by that terminology, so let me explain.

When the Great Commission was given, it was not simply to inspire believers to go worldwide to witness. As Christians, we often err by emphasizing only the opening part of Christ's command and ignoring the rest. Consider that the commission to go into all the world and preach the gospel is followed by a comma, not a period. In other words, the "go ye" segment was not a complete thought but rather part of a complete thought. The remainder of the verse tells us we are to baptize the converts. And indeed, some teaching must take place for the new believer to understand why he should be baptized and how he is to be baptized.

Then the passage tells us to teach them to observe all the things Christ commanded us in the Bible. How can they observe His precepts and commandments if they are not taught what they are? This teaching is where pastors come into God's plan of global dominance as found in Ephesians 4. Through their shepherding and teaching, they perpetuate the churches that have been started.

These local gatherings, which resulted from obedience to His commission, were later called *churches*, meaning "assemblies"—a Greek term that signified what they would call a *town hall meeting*. That is to say, it was the act of a group of like-minded people in a local area meeting together for a purpose. In the church's case, the purpose was to worship Christ, teach His Word, sing His praises, and multiply into new congregations by repeating the process until all the world has had the chance to both know Him, follow Him, and become a part of one of His local assemblies.

So, you see, a church plant is an assembly of newly saved and baptized believers meeting together regularly for worship under a pastor's leadership. It has nothing to do with renting a facility, buying chairs, installing a P.A. system, printing brochures, and announcing a starting date. That's how a corporation is started—not a church. Planting a church is like birthing a baby; it takes love and patience, and then the baby will come when it's ready, and not until then.

Points to Ponder

- There are still places in the United States that are void of a good congregation. Any scattered, abandoned babies already there need nourishment as well as those waiting to hear the gospel. Are you able to help start a new church? Do you know where one is needed?

- Are you beginning to see the genius in God's simplistic method of planting new churches? We all have our part to play. If we play well together, new churches are birthed, matured, and reproduce. If we don't play well and all want to do the other's part and not our own, we will struggle to survive, and there will be no grandchildren to carry on His name. Already, over 5,000 American churches are closing every year. How secure is yours?

Where We Fall Short
in Missions

Episodes 3, 20, 32, 37, 43, 44

What Good Is Translation Without Distribution

EARLY MISSIONARIES OF our era understood that they could not make a lasting impact on the citizens of their lands, whether they be the curious or the converted unless the people had the Word of God in their own language. Many famous missionaries spent much of their time in translation work. Adoniram Judson translated and went to prison to preserve the Burmese Bible. Henry Martyn and his partner, John Marshman, translated the New Testament into Hindi and Persian. They oversaw and assisted in the translation of the entire Bible and Bible portions in seven languages.

In 1925, author David Brown wrote of their efforts and zeal in producing Bible translations. He acknowledged that with some languages, their translations stand "unrivaled." In contrast, other translations were "put to the press without knowing a word of them or being able to read the characters in which they are written."

Other missionary translators, unknown or little remembered by modern man, now live eternally as legends in heaven, having translated God's Word in the languages of the empires, societies, and even the small tribes they served. Like the early British missionaries to the American Indians, many translators gave their lives to translate the Bible into languages that are no longer spoken. Still, those who spoke their tongue in those days now abide in heaven forever.

Jewish scholars believe that Moses wrote in Egyptian, Job wrote in Akkadian, and Solomon translated the Scriptures into many languages, including ancient Hebrew. After the division of Israel, much of Judah spoke Sumerian, and Daniel later translated Scripture into Chaldean, Sumerian, and Persian. Finally, Ezra later translated it into "modern" Hebrew. From the works of Daniel and Ezra, the Greek Septuagint was eventually compiled and used by Jesus in His earthly ministry.

Whenever and however they accomplished it, the early missionaries understood and agreed on the urgency of translating the Bible into the various languages of their day. So, why don't we feel the urgency of distributing it to our world in our day? When did giving out God's Word cease to be important to us? And why?

At Final Frontiers, we spend enormous efforts and resources providing a copy of God's Word to pastors and believers who do not have one, especially in Islamic countries. We hope you will join us in this great adventure.

Points to Ponder

- Does it surprise you that Carey would print Bibles he could neither read nor verify their correctness? Most missionaries would agree that while we prefer correct translations, an inadequate one (for now) is better than nothing at all. Is that hard for you to accept, or do you agree?

- In your opinion, was it time wasted for missionaries to translate Scripture for languages that no longer exist?

- If versions and translations are so important to us, why do you think we don't emphasize printing and distribution? What good is a Bible sitting in a case inside a warehouse?

Making Converts
in Our Image

A FTER HIS DEPARTURE, Paul wrote to the churches that false teachers had infiltrated and misled the believers. He had taught a doctrine of salvation by grace alone, and in his absence, they were imposing their doctrine of works by keeping Jewish religious laws. These false teachers realized they could not stop Paul or dilute his zeal, so they changed their tactics by following him, sometimes perverting, sometimes denouncing his message.

The false teachers caused the recent Greek and Celtic converts of the Galatian churches to doubt their salvation over circumcision. Paul grew so upset that he wrote in Galatians 5:12 that if these teachers want to require *circumcision* (the cutting away of the flesh), he wished they would go "all the way" with their heresy and set an example by actually castrating themselves. In our day, circumcision is no longer an issue, but as missionaries, we do understand the frustration caused by teachers following behind us who subvert our teaching.

Among our evangelical brethren, divisions are not usually made over doctrine but rather over opinions and twisted interpretations that we disguise as doctrines. Such matters as dress style and music preferences tend to divide our churches and dilute our zeal, shifting our fervor from evangelism to non-essential preferences. As a boy, my pastor taught it was a sin to work on Sunday, but was his preaching not work for him? And what about going out to eat after church? The restaurant employees had to work for him to eat. We pervert God's Word when we insert our interpretations. We preach personal preferences as doctrine and judge those who disagree as liberal, spiritually immature, or sinful. No wonder our mature members leave, seek greener pastures to graze on.

Eventually, our message will be overcome by others who teach biblically validated doctrine. Teaching our preferences as if they are God's Word is *perjury*, i.e., claiming He said something He did not say. Missionaries sometimes unwittingly teach the preferences of their culture as doctrine in other cultures. Doing so can be extremely damaging.

So then, the Great Commission involves more than just soul winning. We are to preach and make disciples, not in our cultural or national image, but His.

Points to Ponder

- Does Paul's tone in suggesting castration surprise you? It seems "un-Christlike" to have such a response, but Paul emphasized his anger at those who hurt the sheep by feeding them poison.

- As parents, we may have ten children, but we delight in the uniqueness of each while expecting obedience from all.

- How has teaching preferences as doctrine affected your family and relationships?

- How did Paul correct false teachings? Can you give an example? (hint: the Epistles)

An Overlooked Command

W E OFTEN SEE the Great Commission as our generalized marching orders, telling us to go but not where to go. That is because we misunderstand the word *nation*. If we accept it to be a synonym of the word "country," then the Great Commission has long since been fulfilled—that is, until a new "country "is born. But when we understand that the word given by Christ was not "country" but *ethnos*, meaning "people, tribal, ethnic groups, or clans," then we realize our task is not yet finished. But why?

Out of 195 countries, 30 percent of all Independent Baptist missionaries live in only five. Because so many missionary families are clustered together, 72 countries are without even one missionary family. Why would God tell us to go to *all* the world then only call us to a few countries? Because for the most part, He calls us to a people—not to a country. Let me explain:

With 206 families, Mexico has the second-largest number of missionaries. Most, if not all, were trained to reach only those speaking Spanish. But scores of other ethnic groups are living there who do not speak Spanish.

For example, 22 percent of the population—over 28 million souls—identifies as being *indigenous* and not Mexican! Of these 28 million souls, 64 languages are recognized as indigenous. This number includes 17 tribes with more than 100,000 people and 47 other tribes or clans with fewer. Yet, for the most part, if some devoted missionary finds and evangelizes just one of these tribes, it is not because he was taught they were there; it is because he either stumbled upon them or heard of them and intentionally sought them out.

God told us to go everywhere, so I wonder why He would seemingly call so many missionaries to one country and none to others. Either many missionaries are not going where God intended them to go, or those God intends to go are not going. Also, though we go as *missionaries* in name, we almost always go as *pastors* in practice. It's difficult, even impossible, for a pastor to move from place to place continually, but Paul taught us that doing so is imperative for a missionary. How else will the entire world hear the gospel? Sending missionaries to act as pastors may seem like a good plan; it's just not God's plan.

Points to Ponder

- It's logical that if a missionary serves as a sedentary pastor, he cannot plant new churches. So why is he there? What is his calling? What is he supported to accomplish?

- Why do you think missionaries cluster rather than going to more countries?

- List the five counties where 30 percent of our missionaries live. [Answer: Brazil 253, Mexico 206, the United Kingdom 112, the Philippines 118, and Canada 104.]*

*Source: Missionary Gil Anger, *www.reachingbeyondborders.org;* 2010.

We Can't Reach
Those Who Have Passed On

I LOVE HISTORY. Whenever I have an opportunity, I enjoy look-ing at old photographs and observing the fashions, technolo-gies, and architecture of past generations. But most of all, I love to study their faces. I find the facial expressions of young and old, the tender and the weather-beaten fascinating. In their eyes, I can see some engulfed in the delight of their day, and others are immersed in grief that seems overwhelming. Some have smiles, some tears. Some are as mundane as an old, wrinkled cowboy leaning against the chuck-wagon's wheel while drinking a cup of coffee, and others as traumatic as a wartime massacre of mangled corpses and faces, forever frozen in the excruciating agony of death's grip. But no matter the photo, one question always invades my thoughts; I can't help but wonder if that person, now in eternity's domain, knew Jesus as his Savior.

We know that it's too late to tell them about Jesus, give a personal witness, or send a missionary to their jungle hut, their prairie farm, or their city slum. Time has removed them from our reach. We will only see their faces again in heaven's courtroom. The truth is, all we can do, is attempt to reach those alive in our day. Doing so is neither a small task nor, once completed, an insignificant one. Why? Because statisti-cally, more than half the people who have ever lived are alive today.

What does that mean? It means that you and I have the opportunity to reach more than half of all the men, women, and children who have ever lived.

Whatever failure our forefathers may have allowed, whatever the lack of zeal that may have hindered them, whatever greed for temporary riches may have distracted them, those who have passed have passed hopelessly. How many were they? Only God knows, but of all the people who lived from AD 30 till today, 67 percent never heard the name of Jesus or His gospel.

We must have two goals in missions. First, we must specifically target those who have never heard His gospel. And second, we must teach all believers in every church in every country to do the same.

Points to Ponder

- How many generations of your forefathers knew Christ as Savior?

- What steps are you taking to ensure every generation that follows you will hear?

- Can you find a people group somewhere in the world and make it your responsibility to get the gospel to them? We have national church planters living near many of them. They have the message but lack only the fuel to get to them. (Check out www.joshuaproject.net)

The Greatest Commandment and the Great Commandment

J ESUS NOT ONLY gave us the Great Commission, but He also gave us the Greatest Commandment: *"Thou shalt love the Lord thy God with all thy heart, and with all thy soul, and with all thy strength, and with all thy mind; and thy neighbor as thyself"* (Luke 10:27). The commission and the commandment are codependent.

Before departing for heaven's glory, our Lord was surely aware of the welcome that was awaiting Him. By whatever means heaven celebrates, whether it be cake, balloons, or fireworks, you can be sure the angels had prepared a celebration unlike any they had ever had before. Christ was about to be received back in all His glory. The Son of God was going home! Heaven's Darling was about to greet His Father and be adored by His creation. What excitement, what anticipation He must have had.

Yet, at such a moment, He gave a departing order to His followers— one that would put the icing on the cake of His earthly ministry. His directive was for them to go, preach, baptize, and teach their converts to repeat the process in and for every coming generation perpetually. To be sure all present and future followers would do it correctly, He left the task in the capable hands of those whom He loved and trusted, arranging for the very Spirit of God to anoint their ministry, just as He had anointed Christ's. He equipped them, declaring that all the power He had used to create the universe was now theirs. By their obedience, they would demonstrate they loved the Lord their God with all their heart, soul, strength, and mind. By evangelizing their neighbors and beyond, they demonstrated that they had the same love for others they had for themselves.

The Great Commission and the Greatest Commandment are inseparable. If we love God, we will obey Him. If we love others as we love ourselves, we will warn them of their impending eternal doom and eagerly introduce them to the gospel of Christ. But if we ignore His Great Commission, then we also ignore His Greatest Commandment. Our inaction now declares that we choose to someday stand before God in disobedience. We may love Him then, gazing on His glory, but we certainly didn't love Him while mortal...nor did we love our neighbors as ourselves.

Points to Ponder

- We think of our celebration in heaven as being joyful, but I wonder if guilt for our deliberate failures here will cling to us for a time there. After all, there will be tears there for Him to wipe away.

- Imagine for a moment the glorious grand entrance Christ must have made. If the return of the prodigal son produced such celebration, imagine the return of the Perfect Son.

- How does your life indicate to observers which of the commands you consider to be the greatest command?

Be Warmed and Fed,
but Not by Me

J AMES, THE PASTOR of the church in Jerusalem, was perhaps the
first pastor in history, and he was also the younger brother of
Jesus. Christ trained the disciples for a few years, but James lived with
Him most of his life. Imagine what he learned from his older half-
brother—both by speech and example. Perhaps this is why James tells
us that pure religion is demonstrated, not by theological education or
position, but by caring for the widows, orphans, the incarcerated (usually unjustified in that day), and the needy.

He revealed the self-righteous hypocrisy of the so-called religious
class by scolding them for their inaction. He said to them, "Though you
have an ample wardrobe, you see the naked and say to them, 'God bless
you; I'll pray you receive some clothes,' but you send them away still naked. You see the hungry and say, 'God, bless you, I'll pray God sends you
food,' but you send them away, still hungry, knowing that your kitchen
pantry is overflowing." In essence, they were saying to the needy, "I pray
God sends someone to clothe you and feed you—just not me."

We like to read this passage because it makes us feel more spiritual
than the hypocrites He rebuked. But I must wonder why James mentions only two categories: food and clothing. Are they the only categories by which we should demonstrate our faith by our works? I believe
this principle applies to every area of our lives (providing health-care

assistance, paying a bill for the unemployed, babysitting for a single mother at work, etc.). If I pray for your need to be supplied while ignoring that God has already given me the ability to supply it, am I not as guilty as those whom James rebuked? What about you?

At our bedsides and in our church pews, we pray for lost souls, for our families, our jobs, our country, and missionaries, but when given a chance to apply the *works of giving* to our *prayers of faith*, why do we falter, giving little or nothing at all? The apostle John also knew Jesus well, but where James made a statement on the subject, John asked a question: "If you possess worldly goods and seeing a brother in need, don't help him; how can you claim the love of God lives in and through you?" (I John 3:17).

Points to Ponder

- Many church members pray for missionaries while never giving to help. They make pledges to the church's missions fund but never fulfill it. Of what value is that prayer?

- Never pledge without fulfilling it. Never delay fulfilling a pledge you can pay today.

- Is there someone in your church who has a physical or a financial need you can meet? Why not volunteer to care for it? Imagine the blessing you will be. Imagine the example it will give your children.

- When it comes to helping others, remember, *wants* are not *needs*. If they could have fulfilled their own needs but wasted the funds elsewhere, theirs is not a need you should bother with.

- What need has someone met for you?

Thoughts on Traditional Views of Missions vs. Biblical Views

Episodes 13, 17, 22, 24, 26, 39

Getting There Is Not the End; It's the Beginning

To an outsider who does not understand church missionary protocols, it would seem that the primary purpose of supporting missionaries is to get them to the mission field.

Missionaries typically announce what percentage of support they have raised so far but rarely tell you the amount of funds they plan to raise. They then tell you what they plan to do once they finally raise the needed support. It's not what they tell us that concerns me, but what they don't tell us.

When a missionary says, "I have "x" percent of my support raised, and as soon as I get the rest, we are leaving," then the inverse of what he is saying is if for some reason he does not get the rest of the funds he is seeking, then he is not leaving—he's staying home. But the purpose of giving to missions is not merely to get the missionary to the field; it is to fund him to preach, disciple converts, plant churches, and train pastors—once he gets there.

As missionaries, we are taught to market our ministry to churches by using flashy videos or photos of cultural landmarks, unusual scenery, professional displays showing native trinkets, local currency, and items of interest from the land we plan to go to.

But most churches where we present our calling don't realize that of all those who start on deputation, up to 43 percent will never finish it. I guess that answers the question about what they will do if they don't raise the desired amount. Perhaps if churches valued experience over good intentions and required a period of internship to be approved and supported as a missionary candidate, those statistics would improve.

Funding missions should be a joint venture between an experienced missionary and the families and churches that support him. Just getting him off the plane at his destination is not the end—only a good beginning.

Points to Ponder

- How many men do you know whom your church supported that never made it to the field? If your answer is none, don't be surprised because that failure is usually considered unnecessary to expose to the churches. Pastors do not want to embarrass the missionary candidate.

- When missionaries raise support, they are raising both "personal" (or family) support and "ministry" support. This drives the amount needed higher than most church members and pastors make. To ease the shock, the missionaries are taught to use percentages rather than amounts.

- Typically, what do you learn about the country, people, or the missionary family by looking at their displays? Are they informative aids or interesting trinkets?

Missionary Life Spans Have Changed

I N THE FIRST hundred years of missionary expansion from Great Britain, the average life span of a missionary was only six years. The average was that long only because one missionary managed to survive 17 years, throwing off the curve. Death for missionaries and their families was so certain that when missionaries boarded their ships to leave England, they packed their belongings, not in shipping crates, but in caskets—one for each member of the family.

Family and friends would walk them to the docks singing meaningful and favorite hymns, crying and waving as their ship faded into the distant curvature of the globe, never expecting and barely allowing their minds the hopeful thought of ever seeing their loved ones again. Many died on board ship after only several weeks of travel before reaching the western coasts of sub-Saharan Africa.

Africa at that time was called the "dark continent" and the "white man's graveyard," referring to the inevitable death from a host of tropical diseases that were so common in the stagnant air of the jungles. Indigenous people endured such diseases at significant risk, but foreigners had no natural immunity and were quickly overcome. Missionary societies eventually forbade their missionaries from venturing into Africa's interior, forcing them to live only and always along the "cooler" coastal regions, where they could live longer and healthier. David Livingstone gained international acclaim because he left the mandated coasts for the interior and made contact with a host of unknown tribal groups that were yet to be reached for Christ. In doing so, he also solved the millennia's international mystery regarding the source of the Nile River. He later died of malaria and dysentery.

Like many others, I have personally endured malaria, typhoid, zika, chikungunya, dysentery, influenza, food poisoning, altitude sickness, venomous bites, and a host of other diseases and ailments. Still, due to advances in medical care, missionaries today can live longer and healthier, being enabled to preach for years beyond those anticipated by our noble predecessors.

Points to Ponder

- Consider that the early missionaries had no anticipated furlough; due to death or extended travel times, few even made it back home to see their families. This prospective future caused many parents to fear their children would want to become missionaries. That same fear, though now mostly unfounded, still exists in many families.

- Can you imagine the steadfast conviction and zeal that would lead men and women in that era to become missionaries?

- Even today, those who serve as missionaries continually leave behind what they know for what they don't know. They deserve your prayers, respect, and support, whether they be foreign missionaries or national missionaries.

There Is a Difference
Between a Burden and a Call

IN 1967 AT THE age of 11, I felt a call to missions. One year later, that feeling was directed toward the closed country of Russia. By the time I was fifteen, I had memorized Russia's major cities, rivers, roads, and alphabet. I carried a map of Russia in my pencil bag to school every day to study it. At age seventeen, I wrote to Brother Andrew, author of the book *God's Smuggler,* volunteering to work for him. He accepted my appeal but told me to first go to Bible college.

Obediently, I stopped my application process to a university in Moscow and enrolled in Hyles-Anderson College to prepare spiritually for life in Russia. Since then, I have traveled around the world more times than I can remember and have been to over 50 countries, but I have never been to Russia. Did I abandon the call of God? Not at all! God was using the country of Russia to teach me the difference between a temporary *burden* and a lifelong *calling.*

As a teenager, my mother read about John and Betty Stam and wanted to be a missionary to China. She wanted to emulate their self-sacrifice and help the people of China even before she had accepted Christ. After receiving Christ in his late twenties, my dad also wanted to be a missionary but felt he lacked the faith. He did, however, become an ordained pastor at the age of 71 and traveled with me to several foreign fields. Even on his deathbed when I considered backing out of a scheduled trip to India, he insisted that I follow God. He said he would be ashamed if he were the cause of my failing God. Our gracious Lord allowed me to go and return before he passed. Did my parents fail God? No, at all. They loved God so much they wanted to give Him the greatest gift they could—*themselves*. They believed the ultimate service is that of being a missionary. Perhaps you feel that way too. However, by not becoming missionaries, they did what God wanted them to do instead of what they wanted to do for Him. They raised four sons; three are missionaries and the other supports missions. Over half their grandchildren are missionaries, and no doubt generations yet to be born will be as well. No, they didn't fail; they triumphed!

We each need to discern the difference between a burden and a calling. Don't criticize yourself for not doing what God never intended you to do.

Points to Ponder

- A *burden* is "a temporary motivation often interrupted by other burdens." Personality, exposure, and interests affect your burdens. A *call* is "a mandate on your life having nothing to do with motivation or exposure." God calls you to be a missionary; you don't call yourself. He gives you a burden to go to a specific place where you can reach specific people. Then you fulfill your calling by receiving new burdens for new peoples.

- If you wonder if God wants you to be a missionary, relax. He doesn't. If He did, you would not wonder.

- So many "missionaries" fail to get to the field or stay on the field because God did not *call* them; they volunteered because

God Called You Where?

O NE OF THE most common misconceptions in missions is that God calls you to a place. I know what you are thinking: *what about Paul's call to Macedonia?* What about it? In his vision, Paul did not see a *map* of Macedonia; he saw a *man* of Macedonia. That man was declaring that the people—not the place—needed spiritual help. You don't evangelize a place; you evangelize a people.

I have often heard men say they feel called to reach the Jews, but they do not follow that call because Israel does not allow missionaries. They don't stop to think that Jews don't solely live in Israel. More Jews live in the United States than in Israel. And more Jews live in Brooklyn, New York, than in Jerusalem. Italy is home to 45,000 Jews. Some 20,000 call Romania home. Argentina is home to 230,000 Jews. Even Iran has 12,000 "leftovers" from Nebuchadnezzar's captivity and today. Macedonia still has 360 Jews who need to be evangelized. In reality, over 20 million Jews are living in over 100 countries.

If God indeed called you to the land of Israel, whose geographical boundaries continually shift, you'll have to go as a tentmaker (a businessman). Still, if He called you to reach the Jewish people, you can spin the globe and go to over half the world's countries to reach them. Even Bahrain on the Arabian Peninsula has 36. Talk about seeking the lost sheep!

India is also closed to missionaries, but more than a million Indians live in South Africa, England and Canada, and more than 3 million reside in the United States. In fact, 29 countries have Indian populations of over 120,000. Probably dozens live within twenty miles of your home, and they speak English. What are you waiting for?

Do you feel called to Mexico? More than 36 million full or partial Mexicans live in the USA. Why not prove your call using a translator or by learning the language and starting a Latino church here before moving there? After all, if you can't do it here, why do you think you can do it there?

Of course, God can call you to a place if He wants. He is God and not bound to our understanding, but more often than not, when God calls, He calls us to a people. Your burden to reach those people should not be limited to where you think they are, but anywhere and everywhere they are. They may be right around the corner. Go!

Points to Ponder

- Why do you think that missionaries tend to say they are called to a place rather than a people? (The only answer I know is tradition, which is how we have been taught.)

- Is there even one missionary example in the Bible who limited himself to one people?

- If Scripture does not suggest it, why do we require it?

Missionaries Who Move

NOTHING CAN CAUSE a missionary to lose support quicker than moving to another field. Some say he must not have known God's will, yet many godly men will pastor a half dozen churches in their lifetime and do so because they felt God led them to each one. So, why the double standard?

Because frankly and biblically, we don't know much about missions. Here's a simple question for you: where do you find a missionary in the New Testament who stayed in only one location his entire life? The answer is—nowhere! You can find some men trained by Paul who were sedentary in their location, like Titus who lived in Crete, but they were pastors—not missionaries. And his task was not to one city but an entire island of villages. Just because a missionary trained you doesn't mean God can't call you to be a pastor.

According to biblical example, if you're not moving from place to place, seeking out communities yet to hear the gospel, converting them, assembling them, and training or finding them a pastor so you can move on to the next unreached community, you are *not* a missionary. You may be doing a great job as a pastor, a teacher, a deacon, or a minister, but your job classification, at least from a biblical perspective, is not that of a missionary.

We have strayed from the purpose for which God appointed missionaries. That purpose is not to pastor churches in communities who know Christ but to plant churches in places that don't. As a result, some men spend their lives with no urgency to expand or solidify their congregation. After all, he is not dependent on their tithe, but on the churches back in America that are providing his support.

I am not saying a missionary has to move from country to country; he could live in one town and still plant churches in hundreds of towns and villages all over the region. I am saying that a missionary moving to a new field is not a sign of his not knowing God's will; it is a proclamation that he is fully aware of and obedient to God's will. If anything, question the missionary who never moves, never plants churches, and depends on his support from America for decades.

Points to Ponder

- Is there even one missionary example in the Bible who limited himself to one place?

- If Scripture does not suggest it, why do we require it?

- Why should a missionary limit himself to one congregation in one land when our Lord told us to go into *all* the world?

- To wow many different places did Paul go? The Bible mentions 44 that we know of. Paul implies many more than that, and tradition tells us he even went to Hungary, Spain and England.

Get Ministry Practice
Before Going to the Field

To be a genuinely successful missionary, is having a degree in missions necessary? Think of those you consider to be the five greatest missionaries of all time. If you are a student of the New Testament and history, your list may include Paul, Barnabas, Silas, Hudson Taylor, William Carey, David Brainard, C. T. Studd, David Livingstone, Adoniram Judson, James O'Fraser, and Henry Martyn. Probably all of these men attended seminary, but it is unlikely that any of them took courses in Missions. Theology and Hermeneutics, yes, but probably not missions courses. So, how could they be considered successful if they didn't have an academic foundation in missions?

The answer is profoundly simple. You can learn about missions in a classroom, but you will only learn how to do missions on the field—by actually doing it. You can also learn about aviation, auto mechanics, or welding in a classroom, but you'll never get hired without experience. That's why most professions have apprenticeships. Next time you have an operation, consider this: do you want a highly educated surgeon or one with education and years of experience?

For the past fifty years in missions, Americans have deviated from the philosophy of "get some training first." Our missionaries go directly to the field with no real apprenticeship at all. Thankfully, being a pastor still requires having some hands-on experience. Imagine if your pastor had no experience pastoring before he took the job. That's why most start as assistant pastors or youth pastors. The title should come only after the education and the apprenticeship.

But in missions, no. We send out young families with no experience to a strange land and expect them to both survive and thrive. No wonder nearly half of all missionaries quit in their first three years. But if they are not to blame, at least they tried. The fault is with the sending churches who sent a novice to do what a veteran would struggle to accomplish. There's a reason why all coaches insist that you don't get to play in the game if you don't come to the practices.

Points to Ponder

- If we understood what missions is, we would understand why a family needs to be apprenticed before being appointed.

- Doctors, financial planners, plumbers, coaches, mechanics, teachers, pilots, electricians, air traffic controllers, train engineers, and even Uber drivers go through internships or apprenticeships. So, why do we look for experience in every field except missions? Is that proper management and stewardship of God's work?

- It is better to be trained in the classroom and tested on the field before titled with a position.
  Education + Experience = Missionary

Postscript

I HOPE YOU have enjoyed reading my thoughts on missions. They were developed over more than three decades of experience. In those years, I have seen many hundreds of churches and thousands of believers have their insight expanded, and their opinions shifted from traditional missions' methods to the biblical example.

Others have not yet been taught what you have read. They are good people with a sincere desire to see the world reached. They look at traditional methods and feel we have done a good job accomplishing the Great Commission. If the lights come on when I flip the switch, I feel the electrician has done a good job too. But I have no idea what the codes are and if he followed them. Someday my house could burn down, but in the meantime, the lights work fine.

There is no logical reason to suspect that God would assign us a task to do without telling us how to do it. If we deviate from His instructions, we will likely burn the house down. If we obey them, we will turn the world upside down in every generation.

I hope my thoughts will illuminate a pathway for young missionaries to follow, older missionaries to adjust, and churches to comprehend how great is the task before us, but how easily it can be accomplished by following His instructions.

I am always eager to speak with missionaries who have questions and churches who want more instruction. I exist to fulfill His Great

Commission and feel we can best do that by supporting national missionaries (church planters) already on the field who are experienced and qualified. If you would join me in supporting them with whatever you can, please visit our website at *www.FinalFrontiers.world*

The Final Frontiers
Great Commission Fund

*How you can have accountable results
with your missions giving*

D O YOU WANT to know how what you give is being used? Final Frontiers has a variety of ministries from which you can choose that are phenomenal.

- Smugglers prints and distributes Bibles throughout the Islamic world.

- Touch a Life sponsors orphanages, children's homes, and feeding centers which you can help for any amount, or you can sponsor a child directly for $35 monthly.

- We also have ministries to the elderly, widows, lepers, the incarcerated, Bible institutes, radio, TV, audio Bibles, etc., to help reach those who have never heard of Jesus.

Our primary ministry supports national church planters, helping them better do what they were already doing when we met them. We support experienced men only, not novices.

You can support such a man for $50 monthly and receive quarterly reports from him to you. Or you can give any amount, in any frequency, to partner with our 28,000+ preachers by supporting the *Great Commission Fund*. And you will receive full-length photos with pictures almost every month.

For us, accountability is everything. Have questions? Contact us.

Info@finalfrontiers.org

About the Author

JON NELMS IS the founder of the Final Frontiers Foundation and Touch a Life Child Rescue Centers. At age eleven, he was called by God to be a missionary, and at age thirty, on the last day of 1986, he was set apart for that task by his church. Since the age of eighteen, Jon has served in various pastoral capacities, beginning as a youth pastor at his home church for Dr. Curtis Hutson. He also worked in large youth ministries and helped plant churches in New York, California, Thailand, India, Honduras, and many other countries.

On a trip to Thailand in September 1986, he became convinced that the best way to reach any people in any land was through the witness and work of their own people whenever possible, rather than the efforts of foreign missionaries who have to struggle with language, culture, and customs. From that enlightenment, based on the book of Acts and Paul's policies, he dedicated his life to raising support for national church planters. At the time of this writing, the more than 28,000 church planters in the Final Frontiers network have started over 391,000 house churches and brought more than fourteen million souls to Christ.

Jon, at age 65, continues to travel the world, finding and vetting more men for support, teaching missions in Bible institutes and colleges globally and American, Canadian, and European churches.

Jon is married to Nolin, a Honduran by birth, and has two children, Daniel and Sara, who, with their spouses, now administer the ministries Jon started. He is also blessed with six grandchildren.

Other Books by Jon Nelms

Available at Amazon.com

The Great Omission

I N HIS BOOK, *The Great Omission,* Missionary Jon Nelms "tells it like it is" by exposing the failures in missions and the reasons behind them as he leads the reader to logical, biblical, and proven solutions, that, if followed, will allow this to be the first generation to fulfill the Lord's Great Commission since it was assigned some 2,000 years ago. Drawing from personal stories gleaned from his 24 years of missionary work around the world, Jon will stir, motivate, and may even upset you. In doing so, he will challenge your conceptions and lead you to consider God's plans and methods that have been laid aside to perpetuate the unsuccessful, unbiblical methods that have handicapped missionaries for centuries. It is not likely that you can even get past the preface without your concept of missions being both challenged and changed.

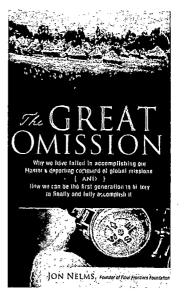

Great Commission Conundrums

GREAT COMMISSION CONUNDRUMS

Solutions to Issues that Hinder Our GLOBAL CONQUEST

JON NELMS

After 24 years of missionary experience, Jon wrote his first book entitled *The Great Omission.* He intended to awaken churches, pastors, and missionaries to the forgotten biblical truth of what a missionary is supposed to be—a church planter and a discipler of pastors.

In recent decades, denominations have redefined a missionary as a social worker, a medical professional, a college professor, or a pastor in a foreign land. This gradual redefining of the term *missionary* resulted from decades of neglect in proclaiming the biblical purpose and practice of a missionary as being primarily a church planter. Thus, in many of our denominations, more men served as a missionary in their home country than worldwide. Jon's teachings on the biblical function of a missionary have reshaped the concept of missions for pastors and missionaries throughout America and worldwide, resulting in a revival of missionary zeal in many men, and thousands of new churches started.

In the following ten years, while consulting with and equipping men in their ministries, Jon faced many conundrums regarding missions and sat down to address some of these in this book, *Great Com-*

mission Conundrums. A glance at the table of contents will undoubtedly illustrate that Jon has both biblical and logical answers to many questions that have puzzled you. The conundrums presented and resolved in this book will help the reader understand the reason for his success.

The Progress Report

Articles on missions, missionaries, national preachers, methods, policies, biographies, etc., can be found in *The Progress Report* archives on the Final Frontiers website.

The Progress Report is a quarterly magazine of the Final Frontiers Foundation available free by post or Internet.

Made in USA - Kendallville, IN
32137_9781736957417
12.15.2021 1624